Microcosm Publishing is Portland's most diversified publishing house and distributor, with a focus on the colorful, authentic, and empowering. Our books and zines have put your power in your hands since 1996, equipping readers to make positive changes in their lives and in the world around them. Microcosm emphasizes skill-building, showing hidden histories, and fostering creativity through challenging conventional publishing wisdom with books and bookettes about DIY skills, food, bicycling, gender, self-care, and social justice. What was once a distro and record label started by Joe Biel in a drafty bedroom was determined to be *Publishers Weekly*'s fastest-growing publisher of 2022 and #3 in 2023 and 2024, and is now among the oldest independent publishing houses in Portland, OR, and Cleveland, OH. We are a politically moderate, centrist publisher in a world that has inched to the right for the past 80 years.

Contents

UNFUCK YOUR BREAKUP

Dr. Faith G. Harper, ACS, ACN

UNFUCK YOUR BREAKUP

Using Science to Heal and Thrive After the End of a Relationship or Friendship

Dr. Faith G. Harper, ACS, ACN

Microcosm Publishing
Portland, Ore | Cleveland, Ohio

UNFUCK YOUR BREAKUP: Using Science to Heal and Thrive After the End of a Relationship or Friendship

First edition - 3,000 copies - December, 2025

ISBN 9781648413711
This is Microcosm # 853
Edited by Lex Orgera
Cover and design by Joe Biel and Sarah Koch
Cover illustration by Lindsey Cleworth

For a catalog, write or visit:
Microcosm Publishing
2752 N Williams Ave.
Portland, OR 97227
All the news from the misfits in print at www.Microcosm.Pub/Newsletter.

*Get more copies of this book at **www.Microcosm.Pub/UnfuckYourBreakup***
*Find more work by Dr. Faith at **www.Microcosm.Pub/DrFaith***

To join the ranks of high-class stores that feature Microcosm titles, talk to your rep: In the U.S. **COMO** (Atlantic), **ABRAHAM** (Midwest), **BOB BARNETT** (Texas, Oklahoma, Arkansas, Louisiana), **IMPRINT** (Pacific), **TURNAROUND** (UK, Middle East, Africa, Europe), **UTP/MANDA** (Canada), **NEWSOUTH** (Australia/New Zealand), **APD** (Asia), **HarperCollins** (India), and **FAIRE** in the gift trade.

Did you know that you can buy our books directly from us at sliding scale rates? Support a small, independent publisher and pay less than Amazon's price at **www.Microcosm.Pub**.

Global labor conditions are bad, and our roots in industrial Cleveland in the '70s and '80s made us appreciate the need to treat workers right. Therefore, our books are MADE IN THE USA.

EU Safety Information: https://microcosmpublishing.com/gpsr

INTRODUCTION

People don't generally come to my books when things are going fantastically well in their lives. This book is definitely no different. You're likely reading it after a fresh breakup, or to prepare for an impending breakup, or you're a nice human wanting to better support someone in your life going through a shitty time.

Since this book is especially for *fresh* grief, I've structured it a bit differently than usual. It consists of little manageable bites on different topics surrounding breakups interspersed with advice shared by other readers. So you can easily dip into whatever you're needing at the moment. Or you can let the universe decide by opening to any page randomly and seeing what you find. You can also read all the way through just fine. It is set up to flow properly from section to section, but it's not a requirement in order to get best use out of the book. Yay for doing whatever is right for you!

Because my books are known for being heavy on the science end, I've still shared all relevant research within each section so you can see exactly what research I am talking about when I discuss decisions about public disclosure, or rebound relationships, or any other various topics.

This isn't a repeat of my grief book, and if you are in the throes of some heavy pain that feels unending, that book might be a really good one for you. Also therapy if that's accessible to you. Throughout this book you'll see me suggest therapy, maybe even more so than in my other books. That's intentional, because we tend to allow ourselves to seek therapy for post traumatic stress disorder, depression, anxiety, and other emotional health issues. And we may not think of a breakup as being an emotional health issue.

You may be just fine and need a little hug and a pep talk from this book, or you may need more support. So the places where I say, "This might be a good place to try a sip of therapy" and you resonate with the situation? Maybe try a little sip of therapy, see if you want more. Oftentimes, breakup therapy is only a few sessions. Just someone to make space for you to process, to ask the hard questions, and to help you get the next season of your life on track. As with the price of everything these days, it may end up being cheaper than a commiseration night out with your friends.

I also put out a call to the internet asking two questions: *What healthy coping strategies did you find the most useful in healing after a breakup?* and *What great advice did you get regarding a previous breakup?* I didn't realize it at the time, but when I started getting responses, I noticed that they were a really good test of the book itself. I got a ton of cool ideas that I interspersed throughout the book to augment my suggestions with real-life applications. And in case you are wondering about how people are credited for their contributions? Everyone chose how they wanted to be credited (first name, full name, online handle . . . no one said keep me completely anonymous, though that was obviously an option, too).

Oh! And one more thing!.

Oftentimes, when discussing interpersonal violence and breakups, we don't talk nearly enough about coercive control and the violence it can lead to. Especially when you are leaving. So beyond just talking about those statistics, I included an appendix with a bunch of information on coercive control and the different forms it can take. Because for many people it feels incredibly fucking normal, especially when it's not coupled with any physical violence.

Listen to any hinky feelings you may be having about your safety around your ex or soon-to-be-ex. And read that section to see if you recognize any patterns that weren't evident to you before so you can be as safe as possible in a potentially dangerous situation.

I wish I could make everyone tea and cookies, and give you a cozy blanket for snuggles, and let you have a good cry and then a nap on my couch after we chat. Unfortunately, I only have a couple of sofas available, but the chat part is here, and you can load up on your own comfort items while you read.

And take care of yourself, ok? You know what I mean, and you know if you aren't doing that. Grief tries to tell us that none of these things matter right now, but they really, really do. So please believe me over your sad brain. Take your time re-engaging in the world if you need to, but take care of *you* in the process. And let the real ones in your life show up for you and do the same. I bet a lot of them also have tea and cookies and cuddly blankets and good listening ears if you are brave and vulnerable enough to ask.

Let's get started.

WHAT IF I'M NOT SURE YET? I STILL NEED TO DECIDE!

Hey there, love bug. For most everyone turning to this chapter first, I am (to quote the cool kids) gonna hold your hands and hurt your feelings: *There aren't many scenarios in which someone is thinking about a breakup with any kind of intensity unless they already know that they need to break up.*

If you are seeking other people's opinions about your relationship, you should pay attention to where that impulse is coming from. What are you hoping to hear from them?

Because people who are content and happy in their relationships don't go looking for validation that they are content and happy. Why would they? No need.

People don't generally try to talk themselves **into** a breakup; we are generally trying to talk ourselves **out** of one.

If you aren't quite ready yet, that's ok. If you are hoping things will get better, I will hope along with you. This isn't me insisting that you set your life on fire without good reason. This is only me saying that if you are thinking you may need to break up, you are quite probably heading in that direction. People in solid, living, healthy relationships aren't working to convince themselves those facts. They aren't defending themselves constantly to everyone around them.

So let's go through the questions you need to ask yourself to be really sure. Actually, it's just two questions if we're getting serious about it:

Are you living in the relationship's potential or its reality?

I don't care what your gender, sexual orientation, socio-economic status, or cultural background is. We have all done this. If you've ever dated or considered dating, you have been drawn in by possibility. Possibility is a gorgeous thing, but you can't build a life with possibility.

Now, that doesn't mean we can't invest in a fixer-upper. We know we are also fixer-uppers in somekindaway ourselves, right? Being with someone who is actively working on themselves? Putting in the effort? Making changes? Taking accountability for when they fuck up? Doing their best to make it right? We are all for that, and in a healthy relationship we are giving each other encouragement in our growth work.

But that person with enormous potential who talks big and acts small? They are staying exactly where they are. At least for now. And they're allowed, right? This is an adult. You can't grow them up through sheer force of will. If things remain as they are, is it still a viable relationship for you?

This is the time for some honest reflection. Did you end up with someone who had goals and dreams and ambitions, and now they are flat out on the sofa playing video games all day instead? Are they really, really into you, and you hoped you would feel the same about them over time since they are awfully nice? Have there been ongoing issues that really never get resolved no matter how often you bring them up? Your partner makes a commitment to say . . . spend more time helping you with household chores . . . and the follow-through never happens?

All of these scenarios are ones in which you are living in the *hope of potential* rather than the reality of your relationship's daily life. So that begs the question. If nothing ever changes. If this is just as good as it gets? Is this a relationship that you can continue to live within for decades? Exactly as it is?

If the answer is no, then you do have a real decision to make. One that Cheryl Strayed, in her Dear Sugar columns, refers to as sometimes leading us to a realization that we need to be *brave enough to break our own heart.* Which leads to my second question.

What does done look like?

If you aren't sure yet, or you aren't at the last straw yet . . . what *is* the last straw? This is a process I encourage people to get ahead of because (and this is the other thing I say on the regular) the end doesn't tend to be loud. It's not decided in the heat of battle. Nor should it be, because heat is hot and we yank away to prevent a burn, right? We may know in that moment, but that's generally not the *done* moment.

Done tends to be quiet. Something happens. Something is said or done, and you can hear the relationship break.

We aren't often ready to hear it, so we deny it and go back to our attempts at fixing. But everyone I have ever talked to who has had to call a relationship (yes, myself included) can remember the moment they heard it break. And this is the reason I'm encouraging you to know what *too much* is. To know what done looks like. And it is hardly ever an isolated one-time occurrence that is so egregious that there is no going back. Which means it is incredibly difficult to even give examples of what done looks like. It's patterns of behavior that aren't getting better even when commitments to better are made. Or a continuous disrespect that you are being asked to endure. It's often things that seem an irritant rather than a real problem if explained in isolation from other events. But you heard the break. And you don't have to continue to patch and spackle and spackle and patch something that is crumbling at the foundation.

The decision only belongs to the people living in that relationship. And we don't often trust ourselves to make these decisions. But you know what? Letting others decide or passively continuing to wait for something to change are also decisions. And they are active decisions even if it doesn't feel like that. You are actively deciding to give your power away when it is incredibly important to own it. You will always feel better about a decision you made with thought and consideration—and for yourself. Good or bad, it's always better to manage our own messes, right? Listen to yourself. Make the best decision you can with the information you have. There is far more peace in doing so than letting things "run their course" for time eternal.

PREPARING IN ADVANCE FOR A BREAKUP

A breakup sucks no matter what the configuration. It may include "just" your larger social group and your personal support system. It may also invoke associated legal entanglements (loss of your home, custody considerations, financial considerations, geographical relocations, etc.). But what all breakups have in common is that they include more losses than the relationship itself.

Breaking up is definitely its own skillset, which has even been studied by social science researchers. They found that most people feel confident in their ability to successfully engage in breakup-related tasks. Meaning: knowing when to break up, doing so appropriately, not delaying the inevitable, and accepting if they are broken up with. It's a hallmark of adulting, right?

Though it turns out that nearly a quarter to nearly a half of us aren't great at these respective tasks at all. Anyone who has been out there running these streets can likely testify. Boo just disappears (ghosted), poltergeisted (confirmed date with a no-show *and then* complete ghosting . . . sometimes also called polter-ghosting), you get strung along until they find what they think is better (monkey-branching), and when they act shitty to get you to break up with them (reverse-discarding).

To name a few.

There has always been shit-ass behavior in the dating world. With so much of our lives now lived online, it has gotten even easier to engage in shit-assery. So please. For the love of Pedro Pascal and all other holy beings, don't be a shit-ass.

Now if your ex is dangerous, you are in no way a shit-ass for ghosting them, and more on that in another section. Otherwise? Put on your adulting pants and prove to those researchers you are not in the half of people who forgot how to act right during a breakup.

Break up when you know you need to. I mean, if they are actively in the hospital or something, waiting a minute is fair. But don't drag shit on for months. Be clear and direct. In person is always best, phone call or video chat second best. If you text-message break up, I am sending Liam Kyle Sullivan after you. And if you sticky-note break up, it'll be Carrie Bradshaw. And you don't want to be trolled on YouTube or in a fictional New York newspaper relationship advice column do you?

Have as much of a plan in place as possible. Including what happens next, who you're going to tell, what you are going to tell them, and at least the start of some organization around any legal entanglements (more on that in another section if that's your need).

And if you are being broken up with? No matter how shit-ass they were in the breakup? Accept it and start healing. More on the human need for closure in another section because you may need that

Real-Life Advice

My therapist told me that love on its own isn't enough. Just being loved and feeling loved isn't sustainable for a happy long-term relationship.

—Jennifer M.

The Research

Beckmeyer, J. J., & Jamison, T. B. (2019) "Is breaking up hard to do? Exploring emerging adults' beliefs about their abilities to end romantic relationships." *Family Relations.* Advance Online. doi.org/10.1111/fare.12404

Kitson G. C. (1992). *Portrait of Divorce: Adjustment to Marital Breakdown.* New York, NY: Guilford Press.

Wang H., Amato P. R. (2000). "Predictors of divorce adjustment: Stressors, resources, and definitions." *Journal of Marriage and the Family,* 62, 655–668.

Wickrama K. A. S., Lorenz F. O., Conger R. D., Elder G. H., Abraham W. T., Fang S. A. (2006). "Changes in family financial circumstances and the physical health of married and recently divorced mothers." *Social Science and Medicine,* 63, 123–136.

tap tap

GHOSTING

Modern society has made ghosting far easier in some ways (block block block delete and block) and more difficult in others (most everyone is findable and traceable online . . . no moving to Montana and changing your name). The term itself does come from the rise in online dating and social media platforms making it easier for people to avoid in-person conversations and confrontations, eventually becoming so prevalent a behavior that it got added to the Merriam-Webster dictionary in 2017.

Ghosting refers to the act of ceasing contact with someone, unexpectedly and abruptly,though there may be some early signs that it's on the horizon with people who begin to share less, respond less, and show up less. While ghosting originally related to dating, it quickly spread to any relationship where the other party just dips on the relationship with no explanation.

Is it a shitty thing to do? Almost always. Kind honesty and forthrightness is always the preferable interaction. Not just for the person who is getting dumped (ghosted) but also for the dumper. Because if you don't have the guts to be honest about your feelings you never grow as a person. It's immature behavior, and we are here to act grown. You don't have to go into a big long monologue, and you definitely don't have to do a deep dive into your reasons why. But say something. Say, "Thank you for inviting me out! I enjoyed getting to know you, but I don't see us being a long-term match, and I want you to go find the person who does."

If there was a problem to address you can mention it, without making it a huge discussion point because if you decided you're done, you don't need to spend time defending your doneness. Maybe it's "I had a problem with how you treat waitstaff. I was uncomfortable and don't see myself continuing a relationship with someone who isn't respectful to service workers. Best of luck to you in the future!" They will either hear you and change something or continue being an asshole to service workers. Either way it is no longer your issue to manage.

Does it make you sound like the lady from HR telling you to pack up your desk? Kinda, yeah. But it's better than leaving someone hurt and confused.

All that being said, if someone is truly dangerous? And ghosting them allows you to better protect yourself? Then by all means, be as spooky as you want. Cut off contact, block them everywhere, don't respond to attempts to get through (and collect any evidence of them trying to stalk or harass you in case you have to get a protective order). If someone is dangerous and violent or even if your gut is telling you they might be? Security specialist Gavin de Becker posits that we are taking in and sifting through enormous amounts of information at a preconscious level and that leads to our bodies responding to what our brain didn't process through our prefrontal cortices. So your gut is telling you to get all the way the fuck out: Listen and protect yourself.

The Research

Daraj, L. R., Buhejji, M. R., Perlmutter, G., Jahrami, H., & Seeman, M. V. (2024). "Ghosting: Abandonment in the Digital Era." *Encyclopedia, 4*(1), 36-45. https://doi.org/10.3390/encyclopedia4010004

De Becker, G. (2021). *The Gift of Fear: Survival Signals That Protect Us from Violence.* Back Bay Books, Little, Brown and Company.

Freedman, G., Powell, D. N., Le, B., & Williams, K. D. (2024). "Emotional experiences of ghosting." *The Journal of Social Psychology, 164*(3), 367–386. https://doi.org/10.1080/00224545.2022.2081528

Navarro R, Larrañaga E, Yubero S, Víllora B. "Psychological Correlates of Ghosting and Breadcrumbing Experiences: A Preliminary Study among Adults." *Int J Environ Res Public Health.* 2020;17(3):1116. doi:10.3390/ijerph17031116

Park, Y., & Klein, N. (2024). "Ghosting: Social rejection without explanation, but not without care." *Journal of Experimental Psychology. General, 153*(7), 1765–1789. https://doi.org/10.1037/xge0001590

Thriving Center for Psychology (2025, April 9). "Report: Top 6 Reasons Gen Z and Millennials Ghost." Thriving Center of Psychology. https://thrivingcenterofpsych.com/blog/gen-z-millennial-ghosting-statistics/

SIGH ...

YEP, THAT'S A COMMON SIDE-EFFECT OF DATING. GOOD NEWS IS IT'S TOTALLY TREATABLE!

BREAKUPS ARE HARD NO MATTER WHAT: WHAT RESEARCH SHOWS US

All breakups are hard. Even if we weren't married, planning on getting married, living together, etc. Even if we are the ones that initiated the breakup. Because hardly anyone gets into a relationship planning on it not working out, unless it's Leonardo DiCaprio staring down the 26th birthday of his current girlfriend. The big thing that shows up in the research time and time again is that breakups pretty universally come with psychological distress and lower life satisfaction. There aren't any differences in this based on what caused the breakup. Like, it's not worse if someone was caught cheating or relapsed or whatever.

The effect of breakups isn't any different in the modern era based on gender lines either. Before the 1970s, women reported worse effects, but there was a big change from the

70s to the 90s. Starting in the 70s, women weren't reporting worse breakup effects than men anymore. The Equal Credit Opportunity Act was passed in 1974 and the Sex Discrimination Act was passed in 1975. So my guess (but y'all know I'm right) is that the gender differences around breakups in the past were related to the fact that women were very likely to be completely financially fucked if they were dumped. And now we are far more likely to have our own money and resources. And even if we don't, we have more avenues for going and getting them.

Specifically, research shows that having been cohabitating and having had plans for marriage were associated with larger declines in life satisfaction after a breakup. I mean, yeah, we all know that but science agrees. Interestingly, having higher relationship quality was associated with *smaller* declines in life satisfaction following a breakup. There aren't, otherwise, any other factors that make some breakups worse than others, like the reason for the breakup.

Breakups suck because they suck. For everyone.

The Research

Forbes Magazine. (2023, May 15). "When could women open a bank account?" Forbes. https://www.forbes.com/advisor/banking/when-could-women-open-a-bank-account/

Rhoades, G. K., Kamp Dush, C. M., Atkins, D. C., Stanley, S. M., & Markman, H. J. (2011). "Breaking up is hard to do: the impact of unmarried relationship dissolution on mental health and life satisfaction." Journal of family psychology :

JFP : journal of the Division of Family Psychology of the American Psychological Association (Division 43), 25(3), 366–374. https://doi.org/10.1037/a0023627

Sprecher, S. (1994). "Two sides to the breakup of dating relationships." Personal Relationships, 1(3), 199–222. https://doi.org/10.1111/j.1475-6811.1994.tb00062.x

FRIEND BREAKUPS MIGHT BE EVEN WORSE THAN ROMANTIC ONES

Only recently have behavioral scientists started researching friendship breakups. Weird, right? Because we have definitely been researching friendships themselves and have used the data to demonstrate how incredibly important friendships are across our lifespans. Friendships are associated with better physical and emotional health, including our satisfaction with our lives and our view of our own well-being. One study demonstrates that as we get older, friendships are a stronger predictor of our well-being than our families.

If they are so important, why is there so much romantic breakup research and so little friendship breakup research? Friendships tend to be very flexible relationships. We all have that one bestie who we may not see or speak to on the regular, but we know they'd roll up for us if we needed them.

And then maybe they don't show up when you need them. Or we let so much time pass, we don't even consider asking them for help. The friendship suffocated at some point along the way, and we didn't even notice. In fact, a friendship passively just fading off (instead of an active, acrimonious blowout) is the norm.

Another problem we don't really consider is that friendships end as often as romantic relationships do. And when they do end? We don't really talk about it. If bae dumps us, we feel a sense of social permission to not just grieve but grieve with the support of others. But with friendships, we feel like we don't have that same permission, and we end up both sad and isolated when we lose a friend.

Since breakups have social norms attached to them, we are also far more likely to discuss the breakup parameters with a romantic partner than with a friend. Like, how do we handle our mutuals? What happens if we end up at the same party? Are we still going to cover for each other with our shitty boss?

If we aren't talking about any of this as a society, it means we are slower to talk about it research-wise. But we are getting there and starting to unravel some of the contextual factors surrounding friendship breakups and the personality characteristics that impact our decision-making. For instance, what makes someone more or less likely to end a friendship? Their own value system and whether they value maintaining friendships over asserting their own ethical stance or vice versa. Asserters are, unsurprisingly, far more willing to call it over a transgression than maintainers.

Even so, because friendships are so fluid to begin with, how we choose to change the status of that friendship also varies. Another team of researchers categorized these status changes as:

Ending: Terminating the friendship entirely.

Distancing: Having less engagement with the friend, less time together, less contact in general, etc.

Compartmentalizing: Keeping the friendship to one specific "safe" area and/or avoiding a not safe area. Like not discussing work issues with the friend who has been unsupportive of your career goals, as an example.

And I think most of us can relate to having tried distancing and compartmentalizing as options. Like, friend-person has been going through it and has been flaky so I'll invite them to group hangs where if they don't show or they're late or they dip early or any other sundry things it won't matter as much. Etcetera.

And yeah, since the research is pretty nascent, there isn't much that is of enormous help if you are struggling with a friendship breakup. I do think it's helpful to remember that we have some different options if a friendship is going poorly. Even if we are high-ethics people who value their own moral stances over maintaining the comfort of established relationships. The ideas of changing the nature and status of the friendship may help you develop a plan that doesn't necessitate a full friendship termination.

Other than that? They suck almost as fully and with less societal empathy around the situation. And the best suggestions I have about that don't come from the research. They come from being a fellow human. And that is please let yourself grieve as you would any other loss in your life. Find your people who you can talk to. Let your therapist know you're struggling. Give yourself grace about being sad.

Real-Life Advice

I've had two breakups from love relationships and plenty of troubled times with leaving friends, jobs, and cherished career plans as well. Those were also breakups of a sort. My father was a complex person, and not someone who I felt comfortable talking about my problems with, but I think he always wanted to support me, and he reached out with a poem. He gave me a print of the poem "Desiderata" by Max

Ehrmann. I have re-read this countless times, and it has helped me deal with all of the tough times. It might seem hokey or corny to read poems through your rage or your tears, but different lines of the piece have resonated with me over the years. It helps remind me that I'm still standing, and I can cope with whatever-it-is this time, too.

—Lynn H.

The Research

Chopik, W. J. (2017). "Associations among relational values, support, health, and well being across the adult lifespan." Personal Relationships, 24(2), 408–422. https://doi.org/10.1111/pere.12187

Harper, F. G. (2021). Unfuck Your Friendships: Using Science to Make and Maintain the Most Important Relationships of Your Life. Microcosm Publishing.

Khullar, T. H., Kirmayer, M. H., & Dirks, M. A. (2021). "Relationship dissolution in the friendships of emerging adults: How, when, and why?" Journal of Social and Personal Relationships, 38(11), 3243–3264. https://doi.org/10.1177/02654075211026015

Vieth, G., Rothman, A. J., & Simpson, J. A. (2022). "Friendship loss and dissolution in adulthood: A conceptual model." Current Opinion in Psychology, 43, 171–175. https://doi.org/10.1016/j.copsyc.2021.07.007

CONSENSUAL NONMONGOMY BREAKUPS

Of course, not everyone in the world (and therefore not everyone reading this book) was in a monogamous relationship that ended; let's discuss how consensual nonmonogamy configurations may be impacted.

First off, I couldn't find any reliable data on CNM breakups versus monogamous breakups. There are definitely stats out there but mostly on Reddit and blogs written by divorce attorneys. And without attribution. So I'm not sharing them.

There is, however, plenty of data surrounding consensual nonmonogamy that is referenceable. CNM isn't rare. In the U.S., research shows that one in nine people have engaged in polyamory and another one in six desired to. And the research of people in CNM (including polyam) shows that they are as satisfied or more satisfied in their relationships. They are as committed or more committed. They report more joy, less jealousy, and better communication than their monogamous counterparts.

(I taught a class a few years ago on what monogamous couples could learn from CNM folks. The communication that one needs to engage in to be healthy in consensual nonmonogamy relationships serves the health of all relationships . . . not just the ones that involve more people.)

Now, I know there is a lot of disapproval of CNM by the greater culture. And even more skepticism about its viability. So I share those numbers intentionally for anyone who is thinking, "Well of COURSE they broke up, that's ridiculous."

My go-to resource on CNM breakups is the aptly titled *Polyamory Breakup Book*. The *Polyamory Breakup Book* was written by my friend and colleague Kathy Labriola. Her clinical experience is that the issues that cause most breakups in monogamous relationships are the ones most likely to cause breakups in consensually nonmonogamous relationships: Incompatibility around sex or money. Addiction problems. Mental health issues. Abuse. Life isn't getting easier no matter the number of partners you have (although having several may be what's necessary in order to purchase a house in most areas).

One thing that has come up in the research over and over that may also be relevant to our discussion here is the difference in how many CNM individuals experience a breakup. Qualitative researchers have reported time and again that many people experience the breakup as a *change* in the relationship, not so much an *ending*. Many communities value maintaining friendships after the romantic attachment is over. And many people report continuing to honor the relationship for what it was while it lasted, focusing on everything they received from the relationship rather than labeling it as a failure. All of which I think can be an incredibly healthy response when it is an authentic one.

On the flip side, the ending of these relationships may cause more isolation than it would for a monogamous individual. If you aren't able to maintain a relationship with the person in question, that can throw you into chaos with your larger CNM community, and you may feel unwelcome or be told that you are. Because both messy and toxic dynamics exist everywhere, right?

There are also reports of individuals who felt that others, especially among their monogamous friends, didn't recognize the loss as being as devastating to them as it was. For example, you may have considered that partner as a spouse, although you were not legally married to them. And of course any children that they had been involved in co-parenting may also no longer be allowed in their lives, with no legal recourse available (as with any stepparent in a monogamous relationship that ends).

No matter how you experience your breakup, you are deserving of support, and it could be harder to find a clinician who has experience working with CNM relationship configurations. There is nothing wrong with looking for a poly-friendly therapist or coach if you want to get some support in the process. I've worked with many people over the years who were nonmonogamous, kinky, queer, non-cis, or any of the categories of humans we so casually *other* in society. Their identities weren't what brought them to therapy but are integral to their lives (like all identities). They didn't want to have to explain or defend themselves while they worked through their grief, stress, trauma, need for boundaries, or whatever the presenting issue was. And that makes a ton of sense to me. If that's accessible to you, please consider it. And if you have a lovely therapist who is willing to learn more to better support you, and it is a breakup you are working on, tell them I recommend Kathy Labriola's aforementioned book!

Real-Life Advice

This is a much larger Real-Life Advice statement, and that's because therapists talk for a living! When writing this section on consensual nonmonogamy breakups and referencing a really great book, ***Polyamory Breakup Book***, my friend and colleague Kathy Labriola (kathylabriola.com) wrote as both a human who practices consensual nonmonogamy and a therapist working with other CNM folks, I sent her a message asking her if she'd like to add her own Real Life Advice piece. Because she's as generous as she is well-versed, she sent me the following with permission to cut to what I need. But we need all of it, so it stands!

> I have found that for most people, there are four key components of surviving and even thriving while recovering after the demise of a precious relationship: self-care, grieving the loss of the relationship, learning whatever you can from the relationship and the breakup, and maintaining and sustaining your other relationship(s).
>
> First and foremost, self-care is at the top of the food chain. Sleeping and eating are paramount, even if you eat a lot of junk food and even if getting a decent night's sleep requires cannabis gummies or short-term use of over the counter sleep meds or a prescription for Ativan or Ambien. Getting out of the fucking house and seeing friends, getting exercise of any kind (being totally agitated and pacing around the house for hours smoking cigarettes and muttering about your evil ex definitely counts as exercise), getting counseling or going to a CNM support group so you won't drive all your friends bat-shit crazy talking about your ex 24/7.
>
> And give yourself time to grieve, don't beat yourself up for feeling sad and defeated for a while. An end to a precious relationship necessitates mourning the loss of a treasured dream of an ongoing life together, and letting go of that hope can be very painful and usually happens in stages.
>
> And while you are grieving, look back on your relationship through as honest a lens as possible, to learn whatever lessons you can from the current debacle. Did you choose someone who was incompatible with you in

some very important ways, which ultimately made the relationship unsustainable? Did you choose a partner with some serious problems, such as alcoholism or drug addiction, out of control anger issues, narcissism or other untreated mental health conditions, or just plain crappy time and energy management skills that made them a less than ideal candidate for a successful CNM relationship? And it's even more crucial to take a stone cold sober look at what problems and issues you brought into this relationship, that you may want to work on now so you will not make the same mistakes in future relationships.

And while you're at it, pay attention to your other relationship(s), as they need care and feeding, too. Don't keep your head so far up your ass obsessing over how your no-good ex did you wrong or whining over how bereft and love-lorn you are that your remaining partner(s) get so pissed off at being neglected that they decide to bail, too! After a monogamous breakup, you can regress to a state of barely functioning and hide in your room crying and drinking tequila every night after work. But if you are poly, you are likely to have at least one other relationship, which you could easily lose if you become such a hot mess that you ignore their needs for companionship, affection, reassurance, and sex (or if you forget to wash your dishes, pay your portion of mutual bills, or take showers). Let your partner(s) know (early and often) that even though you are in a pit of despondency right now, you love them, you are fully committed to your relationship, you are doing your best to remain present with them, and most importantly, "I will be back to a normal level of functioning in this relationship, and in my life, as soon as humanly possible."

For many people there is an important additional task, which is managing the public relations problems created in a CNM breakup. This usually requires "getting out in front of the story," to counter the unfortunate tendency for everyone else to jump to the conclusion that polyamory was the cause of the breakup (while they would never assume that monogamy was the cause of the demise of a monogamous relationship). The usual narrative of friends, family members, co-workers, and even political comrades is to say things like, "Well, of course you ended up getting divorced, because polyamory never works. I told you this would destroy your marriage!" Many poly folks have written a joint statement and either sent it out by email to family and friends or posted it on their social media, explaining that the nonmonogamous nature of the relationship was not the cause of the breakup and asking for caring and support from their loved ones during this challenging time. Other people simply tell a few key people what the actual cause of the breakup was and ask them to communicate it to everyone else in your mutual circles. This will likely spare you the extra burden of having to defend your polyamorous orientation from the monogamists, who have literally just been waiting and hoping for your relationship to "fail" so they could pounce and gloat over the presumed superiority of monogamy.

– Kathy Labriola

The Research

Gupta, S., Tarantino, M., & Sanner, C. (2023). "A scoping review of research on polyamory and consensual non-monogamy: Implications for a more inclusive family science." Journal of Family Theory & Review, 16(2), 151–190. https://doi.org/10.1111/jftr.12546

Hnatkovi ová, D., & Bianchi, G. (2022). "Model of motivations for engaging in polyamorous relationships." Sexologies, 31(3), 184–194. https://doi.org/10.1016/j.sexol.2022.03.003

Labriola, K. (2019). The Polyamory Breakup Book: Causes, Prevention, and Survival. Thorntree Press.

EMOTIONAL OVERLOAD BREAK: THE STRUGGLE SWITCH

Dr. Russ Harris, an Acceptance and Commitment Therapy expert noticed our human predisposition to struggle with our uncomfortable emotions so much that we make them worse. He termed this tendency the "struggle switch" because a painful emotion seems to immediately turn on our brain's desire to fight this emotion in ways that end up making it so much worse.

You're sad? Your brain says, "If you can't stop feeling sad I'm going to now make you feel sad about your sadness. And maybe now also some anxiety. Or irritability. Let's make our resistance to our own emotions as messy as possible. The struggle switch is *emotional amplification*.

You are in the middle of a significant life change. Even if it was your choice and it's all for the better. And that comes with complicated feelings. Rather than resisting them or piling on recrimination for having them, the best way to manage them is to let them exist for what they are.

When you notice the switch is flipped, or you notice yourself hovering over the switch? I want you to picture yourself getting caught in a downpour. You're out in the middle of nowhere, and the skies just open up. You can fret and run around and look for shelter or cover. You can yell and scream about how much it sucks. You can berate yourself for not bringing appropriate weather gear.

Or you can just get wet.

And I want you to try just getting wet. It sucks. You got blasted with something really uncomfortable. I. It'll suck, but the storm *will* pass. And no point making things worse while trying to resist it.

When you notice the storm, look at the sky (mentally or actually), and say to yourself, "Yep, this is a bad one. Hope it passes soon." Do whatever it is you were doing, if possible. Meaning go to work, cook a meal, take a walk, read a book . . . whatever you can do *and* do sad. If you can't, sit with the storm until it passes. Then take a deep breath, honor what you just sat through, and get back to your life. Start over again and again and again. This is a process that takes *real* strength, and you've got that.

Real-Life Advice

Healing doesn't happen by pushing the pain away. It happens by feeling it. By sitting in the uncomfortable, ugly, gut-wrenching emotions and letting them move through you—without needing to fix, change, or rush them. One of the most powerful things someone ever said to me was: "Stop trying to logic your way out of heartbreak. Your heart doesn't speak logic. It speaks truth, presence, and love." That hit me hard—because for so long I tried to bypass the grief. To wrap it up in productivity, busyness, or "I'm fine." Yet in one of the darkest chapters of my life—sitting on that mountain in Peru, thinking no one would miss me—I realized the only way through was inward.

Breakups, like any soul-cracking loss, are an initiation. Not into "getting over it," but into rediscovering who you are now that life looks different. So the best breakup advice? Feel everything. Don't rush the process. Get support. Trust your intuition more than the outside noise.

And remember: this is not the end—it's the beginning of becoming even more of who you're meant to be.

—Shannon McCaffery

IS THERE SUCH A THING AS A "GOOD" BREAKUP? (THE CLEAN PAIN VS. DIRTY PAIN DISCOURSE)

"Is there such a thing as a 'good' breakup?" is a question I got when I started this book. Good is a pretty vague word and has different connotations for different people. There likely isn't any such thing as a happy breakup. A relief breakup maybe, but not happy. But can it be good as in . . . not shitty and messy?

That we can do.

And in that vein, I think good versus bad breakups can be considered a function of what Resmaa Menakem refers to as clean pain versus dirty pain. In his book *My Grandmother's Hands,* which is an exceptional treatise on what we need in order to heal epigenetic racialized trauma, he talks about how we make even the most egregious harm so much worse in our resistance to facing it head on in order to heal.

Mr. Menakem, a therapist and trauma specialist, denotes clean pain as a choice of integrity over fear. We fear the unknown journey to healing.

Dirty pain is the opposite. It's about denial, blame, and avoidance, which causes more pain, both for ourselves and those we come in contact with.

All pain hurts, right? Pain refers to the experience of physical and emotional distress. Dirty pain is a wound we keep reinjuring rather than caring for so it may heal.

Clean pain, like a good breakup, requires courage and Mr. Menakem, like many a good trauma therapist, notes that somatic techniques are integral to our healing approach. He suggests five anchors when the distress of a situation arises. For the heavy lifting it requires to be our best selves in a breakup, we can use his SNAPS anchor protocol:

SOOTHE: Your broken heart, your agitated mind, your panicked body, especially when you

NOTICE your body responding with distress, care for yourself so you can be proactive instead of reactive.

ACCEPT the discomfort of the situation. Resistance to our reactions make it so much harder to feel and release the discomfort. The acceptance allows you to

STAY present in your body. Whatever helps you remain in the here and now rather than dissociate or, alternatively, ramp up. Whatever remains, you can

SAFELY DISCHARGE with the kind of movement that you can engage in that you enjoy and feels good. Any movement that your body craves (go for a walk, take a dance break, do some yoga, lift weights, weed the yard, scrub the baseboards . . . as long as it is safe for you and your body).

The rest of it? Choosing to remain in your moral center. To be proactive instead of reactive. To make the healthiest decisions possible in a tough situation. You got this. You can't control your ex's behavior and choices about a good breakup, but you can control yours.

Real-Life Advice

The advice I received was that I must grieve the breakup of my marriage as a death. Not just the "death" of the relationship, but also the fact that it lasted so long (thirty years), held so many memories, and still contained hopes and dreams of the future.

The first two I'd already gone through and have, and the last one I was giving up/letting go. Now, instead of being selfless and thinking about the needs of another, I needed to become a bit selfish and turn the focus on me personally. These words were said to me by my closest childhood friend and best man at my wedding.

The most helpful strategy was to stay positive and focus on improving myself—while time heals all wounds (somewhat), the conscious act of improving myself and becoming a better person tomorrow than I am today improved not only self-esteem but outlook on life.

—Barney

The Research

Episcopal Church of Minesota (2023). Resmaa Menakem's 5 anchors. https://episcopalmn.org/sites/default/files/resource/Embodied and Somatic - Resmaa Menakem's 5 Anchors.pdf

Menakem, R. (2021). *My Grandmother's Hands: Healing Racial Trauma in Our Minds and Bodies.* Penguin Books, Limited ; Penguin Random House Distributor.

YOU FEEL WEIRD. YOU'RE GONNA. WEIRD IS NORMAL.

So many things happen to our physical body when we have a relational break. You feel like shit for so many science-y reasons. Let's look at that science for a sec. Being close to another human helps us co-regulate our circadian rhythms. When you go to sleep, when you wake up, when you're hungry and ready to eat? All affected. One study, conducted in 2010, found that when people were told they were rejected, their bodies experienced a parasympathetic nervous system disturbance (measured by heart rate).

Emotional loss also lights up the brain in ways similar to physical pain. As Gabor Maté wrote in his book *When the Body Says No*, when we say we are hurting, we aren't being poetic . . . we are being scientifically precise. A 2001 study of emotional pain and physical pain found the same activation points in the brain during fMRI scans. We also experience biochemical withdrawal effects similar to any other detox. Emotional loss is more complicated in a detox (the mesolimbic dopamine [DA] pathway is affected by both, emotional loss is also mediated by the neuropeptides oxytocin and vasopressin, which are instrumental to our attachment process).

This is all to say, everything that feels super crazy to your body? Isn't at all crazy. It is your entire nervous system needing to metabolize this experience so it can recalibrate to your new reality. All this takes a while. This is also why self-care is no joke. It is vital to your recovery. You need safety and support and kindness so your body can heal.

Real-Life Advice

Movement, it was so beneficial to reconnect with my body following a long-term relationship where I felt like I had lost myself for a while. I did this through running (really the only coping skill I had at the time), and this was a time in my life where I found yoga, and probably cried in every class I went to for the first month! I started to go with a loved one and found a new sense of community and connection in this activity both with others and within myself. I still go to yoga when I am able to so that I am able to engage in reconnection with my body, especially when life feels turbulent. Honesty, I think it was the first time I felt my body, mind, and soul connect and the first time my brain and body felt that it was allowed to slow down and just be. I contribute much of my healing to reconnecting with my body, learning how to somatically process what my body had been carrying, and overall attunement to self.

—Kiwi

The Research

Burkett, J.P., Young, L.J. "The behavioral, anatomical and pharmacological parallels between social attachment, love and addiction." Psychopharmacology 224, 1–26 (2012). https://doi.org/10.1007/s00213-012-2794-x

Gunther Moor, B., Crone, E. A., & van der Molen, M. W. (2010). "The Heartbreak of Social Rejection: Heart Rate Deceleration in Response to Unexpected Peer Rejection." Psychological Science, 21(9), 1326-1333. https://doi.org/10.1177/0956797610379236

Larson, G. (2017, January 3). "Why it's so hard to get over your ex, according to a relationship psychologist." Vox. https://www.vox.com/first-person/2017/1/3/14100360/breakup-survival-strategies

Larson, G. M., & Sbarra, D. A. (2015). "Participating in Research on Romantic Breakups Promotes Emotional Recovery via Changes in Self-Concept Clarity." Social Psychological and Personality Science, 6(4), 399-406. https://doi.org/10.1177/1948550614563085

tic
tic
tic
tic
tic
tic
tic
tic
tic
tic
25

THE RE-CALIBRATION PART? ALSO TAKES A WHILE. THIS IS ALSO SUPER NORMAL.

How long is all of this going to suck? A while, bestie. I'm sorry. But if you are doing all the good things to take care of yourself. Connecting with people, being gentle with your body, nourishing yourself, etc.?

It's still going to take a minute.

I remember the "21 days to change a habit" movement that was huge in the aughts. I worked at an agency that bought the bracelets for, I dunno, some health kick team-building thing? Turns out that the 21 days thing is super wrong and false. That number was based on an observation made by a plastic surgeon named Maxwell Maltz in the 1950s.

He noticed that post-surgery, it took about three weeks for his patients to recognize the difference in their body. Like, to recognize themselves in the mirror again with their new nose. Which sounds about right. Having even my hair color changed (my hairdresser is my 6'6" drag queen friend, I don't argue) takes a minute to recognize when I look in the mirror.

But that's about exchanging one somatic map of our own bodies for another, not about adjusting to a loss. The research on breakups found it is far more in line with the VA's trauma recovery timeline that I wrote about in my book *Unfuck Your Brain*. That's the three MONTH number, not three weeks. And divorces take even longer. They are long and drawn out and awful, and the data there says nearly 18 months are necessary for recovery. These numbers make so much more sense to me, and hopefully make sense for your experiences, too. Doing the work means trusting that the recovery will happen; it's just not going to be near as immediate as an online listicle will tell you.

Also? The data about new habit formation also belies the 21-day timeline, which (trust) we will also be looking at in this book.

Real-Life Advice

Having a healthy morning and evening routine. Allowing myself time to feel, to heal, and to reach out to friends. Talking about and processing it with a therapist and being with healthy friends. Taking it one day at a time. Giving up alcohol. Meditating and journaling daily. These all helped tons.

—Shannon McCaffery

Real-Life Advice

I made a deck of 20 notecards each with positive things about no longer being with him, like things I could now do or focus on. They included: meet cute guys, get a Shih Tzu, sex (we weren't having any), grad school, rap music (he hated it), don't share a bed, have kids, have me-time, go dancing, focus on grades, freedom, friends, rom coms (he didn't like them), work more hours for $$, research, sing (he didn't like my singing), money, Disney World (hated amusement parks), festivals, Golden Corral. I used thumb tacks and put them on my wall in my college bedroom in a 4x5 grid. I then made a second deck of notecards in a different color each with things about him I didn't like. This included: judgmental, lack of intimacy, closed-minded, unaccepting, impatient, manipulative, controlling, toxic, arrogant, unsupportive, aggressive, unloving, mean, obsessed with Japan as a white man?, anime, small penis, no sex, negative, condescending, politics. I put them in a 4x5 grid on the wall next to the other one. I had them on the wall as a reminder for times I was alone in my bedroom and felt like I missed him. I also took pictures of them to look at on my phone if I ever felt sad about not being with him. A friend of mine went through a breakup right after me, and we did the same thing for him and his ex-boyfriend. I think the exercise itself is helpful for reminding oneself about the things that make you unique, what brings you joy, and what you might have been giving up by being with someone unhealthy for you. The negative traits were helpful for the times I felt nostalgic about being with him; reading the list reminded me about the things about him I didn't like and that made me feel bad. I also wrote quotes in silly fonts on three pieces of paper that were on my wall: "I am worth more than this." "Everyone can be replaced" (Everything I thought I needed from him I could find in other people). "The cause of your problems can't also be the solution" (The sadness I was feeling could not be made better by hanging out with the person that made me sad).

—Korra

The Research

Lewandowski, G. W., & Bizzoco, N. M. (2007). "Addition through subtraction: Growth following the dissolution of a low quality relationship." The Journal of Positive Psychology, 2(1), 40–54. https://doi.org/10.1080/17439760601069234

Telegraph Media Group. (2009, October 30). "Divorce takes 18 months to get over." The Telegraph. https://www.telegraph.co.uk/news/uknews/6464020/Divorce-takes-18-months-to-get-over.html

PAY ATTENTION TO WHAT YOU'RE REALLY GRIEVING

This is really important because, as I said earlier, so often what we were grieving wasn't the relationship itself, it was the possibility we saw in it.

There is an expression, coined by Alfred Korzybski, a Polish-American philosopher and engineer, which is this: *The map is not the territory.* This means the stories we tell ourselves (and others) are not a complete and accurate representation of reality. The map is our internal experience of a situation. Our perceptions and our beliefs and our hopes. Maps are simplified and incomplete. The territory is reality with all of its complexities and complications and things we know muddled with things we don't know. And we get in trouble when we confuse the two.

Within a breakup, there is often so much grief around what we wanted and wished and hoped for this relationship to be. For the map we created. And when we find out that the map doesn't match where we are actually standing? Recognizing what is the actual territory of our grief and what was mapmaking will help us heal far faster.

And of course the question is, how the fuck do we do that? Making maps is what brains do. We create cognitive heuristics, or shortcuts, for everything in our life so we aren't having to waste brain power constantly to attend to every situation that we encounter. For instance, the recognition heuristic exists because if we are faced with two items and only know what one of them is? We consider the one we recognize as more valuable. This often works fine. To use the same example again, if we don't know what one thing is, it may not be of particular value to our lives or it would have been something we had already become aware of. Not always, of course, but heuristics are reasonably effective for basic everyday activities.

But more complicated issues (like processing a breakup, say) get harder and harder for us to manage the older we get. Because the older we get, the more likely we are to have a bunch of maps in our pockets at all times. Researchers have studied babies and young children in comparison to older teens and adults and found that small, young humans are far more effective at solving problems than teen and adult humans. Because they haven't created nearly the maps (brain shortcuts) that older humans have.

And brain shortcuts can undermine our healing work, which really demands a more mindful approach. Which, in turn, means invoking *inhibitory control.* It's not a great term, because it does sort of give the impression that you are supposed to self-silence. In reality all it means is our brain's ability to notice when we are engaging in a habitual/automatic response (leaning on a heuristic) rather than looking critically at a situation in order to solve it more intelligently. It's an executive functioning (pre-frontal cortex skill), and some people are better at it than others. Neurodivergent people and individuals with brain-based disorders can often struggle even more with the skill.

Fortunately, a couple of things help. One is exercise (which, yes, is really good for the brain not just the body) and engaging in activities that help you practice and strengthen this skill through strengthening the right inferior frontal gyrus [rIGF] and its connections. This is the part of the brain that helps us organize a sequence of actions so we can proceed smoothly, and researchers have found that we can prompt and change these processes. The more you can disrupt events by catching yourself in a pattern, then doing things differently? The more flexible your brain will be in catching unhelpful heuristics. You can practice this in ways that aren't super complex. For example, do you put on both socks and then both shoes? Or are you a sock-shoe-sock-shoe person? Catch the pattern and do it differently. And find other similar opportunities.

I know, I know. This is a lot of science-y science. Because it is the science-y science that will help you see reality clearly when you really fucking need to most. What happens when you stop relying on the idea in your head about this person and focus on what was actually going on in front of you?

Real-Life Advice

First, I try to recognize what I am grieving exactly. Is it the person, the life we had, the life we were working towards, or my comfort in familiarity? I find usually in a breakup it's the latter two as I've never had a relationship just stop working; it was always a slow decline. The mere act of realizing that I'm more upset about needing to make new goals and routines than I am about what the person brought to the table helps me recalibrate. Yes, I'll miss the good times and the nice things they did, but ultimately once I get over the life I thought I had/would have it's much easier to let the rest of it go.

—Amber Jowders

The Research

Borst, G., Aïte, A., & Houdé, O. (2015). "Inhibition of misleading heuristics as a core mechanism for typical cognitive development: Evidence from behavioural and brain imaging studies." Developmental Medicine & Child Neurology, 57(s2), 21–25. https://doi.org/10.1111/dmcn.12688

Chapnick, P. (1989). "The Map Is Not the Territory." ETC: A Review of General Semantics, 46(4), 352–354. http://www.jstor.org/stable/42579580

Dhir, S., Teo, W. P., Chamberlain, S. R., Tyler, K., Yücel, M., & Segrave, R. A. (2021). "The Effects of Combined Physical and Cognitive Training on Inhibitory Control: A Systematic Review and Meta-Analysis." Neuroscience and Biobehavioral Reviews, 128, 735–748. https://doi.org/10.1016/j.neubiorev.2021.07.008

Diamond A. (2013). "Executive functions." Annual review of psychology, 64, 135–168. https://doi.org/10.1146/annurev-psych-113011-143750

Dippel, G., Beste, C. "A causal role of the right inferior frontal cortex in implementing strategies for multi-component behaviour." Nat Commun 6, 6587 (2015). https://doi.org/10.1038/ncomms7587

Petersen, I. T., Hoyniak, C. P., McQuillan, M. E., Bates, J. E., & Staples, A. D. (2016). "Measuring the development of inhibitory control: The challenge of heterotypic continuity." Developmental Review : DR, 40, 25–71. https://doi.org/10.1016/j.dr.2016.02.001

EMOTIONAL OVERLOAD BREAK: SELF-LED REASSURANCE

Internal Family Systems (IFS) is a form of therapy that encourages us to conceptualize ourselves as living with multiple aspects to our personalities that may show up in different situations. Less like dissociative identity disorder and more like code switching. Like the aspect of you that is protective when you feel threatened or whatever.

As with metacognitive therapy, then, we can recognize that we are more than these aspects. In fact, we are more than all of them combined. Which is a lot of explaining to get to the idea of self-led reassurance. Your anxiety, grief, anger, frustration, overwhelm . . . all of it . . . are experiences you are having. Righteously shitty ones, for sure. But they don't define who you are.

Now, this is not advice on "getting over" your negative emotions. Instead, it is advice about recognizing that no matter how big and overwhelming your emotions feel, you can interact with them in a different way than you are used to.

You can say to that aspect of you that's in pain, "Wow, that's really tough. I'm here to help." And maybe you gently care for that part with a nourishing meal and a healthy bedtime. Maybe you engage in some visualization exercises where you imagine yourself in a cozy and safe space so that part can relax and feel safer. Whatever a kind and considerate human would do for someone who is hurting, you can do for yourself.

If negative self-talk worked, it would have worked by now. If telling yourself to suck it up and get on with it was a viable option, you would have done so successfully. It's not a sign of weakness to be nice to yourself; that simply isn't how the human mind works. But reassurance does. And while hearing it from others is wonderful, so is hearing it from yourself. Sometimes that's the only person we have available. And who better than you to lead yourself to healing? It isn't just other people who deserve your care, after all.

TAKE YOUR PORTION OF RESPONSIBILITY IN ORDER TO RECLAIM YOUR POWER

This is the suggestion I will most likely get some pushback around, but bear with me.

Your ex-person may have been truly heinous. And I am absolutely in no way doing that bullshit thing where you are blamed for abuse perpetrated against you. I don't believe the universe assigns lessons. And I do not believe that you needed to have that experience for your own spiritual consciousness . . . or whatever the fuck those fake gurus say.

I am talking about how, upon reflection, there may be things you missed. I mean love bombing worked on you, and *not* because you're an idiot. But maybe because you had a fucked up childhood and were desperate to be seen and understood.

Maybe there is some work to do on your own trauma history. Maybe there are red flags that you need to pay more attention to in the future.

If you are so fearful of ending up in a bad situation again? This is *exactly* how you prevent that from happening. You learn what to watch for. You learn where your own responses lead when you are attentive to your patterns and habits. Should monsters exist? No. But they do. This is your best defense against them.

This practice also is incredibly helpful if you had a breakup that was upsetting and sad and all of those other things, without a presumption that either one of you is a monster. It's just a sad and bad breakup for everyone involved. If you unspool that timeline and look at your responses (not just theirs) what would you want to do differently in the future?

As an example, were your boundaries too permeable? Did you let your partner do things because they were super important *to them*, and it was tolerable at first? But it continued on and on because, again, it was important to them. And you started to build up resentment. And maybe thought you had to just accept what you had agreed to instead of renegotiating the terms. This is pretty common for most everyone . . . especially for those of us with the types of histories that shaped our people-pleasing skills to a fine point.

And from that point on a few things could happen. You can repeat the pattern of being agreeable to the point of discomfort. Or you can avoid the pattern entirely by never being in another relationship ever again. Or you can engage with the pattern and think proactively about where the line between being a considerate partner turns into an exercise in resentment and frustration-building. And you practice sharing that early on in the future. As in, "I love that you have a great group of friends that you enjoy spending time with. Please go to bar trivia night and have fun. I am exhausted and want to go to bed early. Though if you stop for burgers on the way home, I absolutely want to be awoken for french fries and a chocolate shake." Relationships won't feel like nearly the same minefield if you are increasingly confident that you are your best self within them.

Real-Life Advice

My best friend reminded me to forgive my ex . . . and forgive myself for any mistakes or harm done then move on.

—Patti T.

FIGURE OUT CLOSURE

Whether you were ghosted or not, you may not feel that you got real closure at the end of your relationship. What do we mean by closure? Social psychologist Arie Kruglanski stated that closure is something we value because it is the opposite of ambiguity and confusion. Because closure gives us a much desired "why" answer. He found it to be such a huge motivator for humans that it became part of his framework about the process of human knowledge formation.

Knowing things is a highly valued human state of being. We hateeeessssssss the not-knowing the way Gollum hates anything Elf-made. One study of individuals with a high need for closure found that they *also* had statistically significant increases in systolic blood pressure (which is a measure of the force the heart uses to pump blood to the arteries) and an elevated heart rate when reflecting on their lack of closure. These same people also reported higher levels of psychological distress. And while we all recognize how anger and fear are physiologically stressful, we don't often consider grief as being equally stressful to our systems, especially when it feels *stuck*.

The need for closure is because the human brain craves certainly. It wants as much information as possible in order to make choices about safety. If we don't have that information or we don't understand the information we do have, we have a very strong physiological stress response (as indicated with the BP and heart rate numbers). It's so important to us that we can find ourselves stuck in this need. And then engage in mental gymnastics that are often inaccurate. A high need for closure that isn't being met has been correlated with both a jumping-to-conclusions bias and delusion-proneness.

Meaning, if we don't have the answers our brain will make some up.

And what really sucks? Chances are you are seeking closure in a situation where it isn't available to you. Your broken-upping person isn't forthcoming. Or even available at all. Which means you are going to have to find a way to give yourself closure. If I could make them do it I'd be stupid rich, but I haven't figured out how yet. But I can tell you that the breakup and lack of information surrounding it *is* your closure.

You were with someone who isn't willing or capable of honesty. Which is also important information about that person. When the chips are down, they don't have the courage to be honest. And, babes? *That right there is some serious fucking closure.* You were with someone who lacks courage and your relationship failed due in part to their avoidance of difficulty.

Whatever else you need to give yourself, you give yourself. Write a letter. Angry, sad, whatever. Share it with your therapist if you want, then burn it in your firepit. Clean and smudge your space. Do something for yourself that you've always wanted to do but put off because of your now-ex. Plan the trip they didn't want to go on. Get the haircut you were dying for that they made faces about (but NO BANGS). Spend your next day off reading books and eating chips instead of something productive that your ex preferred. Whatever it takes to reclaim your self. Moving forward as your authentic self is perfect fucking closure. And let's see what your blood pressure says about THAT!

Real-Life Advice

I had imaginary conversations with my ex in order to give myself the closure I needed—closure comes from within and the other person won't be able to tell you what you need to hear to heal. This work allowed me to create the space I needed to heal. Journaling also helped, as did long walks. I also got a tattoo to mark that transition in my life.

– Kim

The Research

Gendi, M., Rubin, M., & Sanatkar, S. (2023). "Understanding the relation between the need and ability to achieve closure: A single paper meta-analysis assessing subscale correlations." *New Ideas in Psychology, 69,* 101007. https://doi.org/10.1016/j.newideapsych.2022.101007

McKay, R., Langdon, R., & Coltheart, M. (2006). "Need for closure, jumping to conclusions, and decisiveness in delusion-prone individuals." *The Journal of Nervous and Mental Disease, 194*(6), 422–426. https://doi.org/10.1097/01.nmd.0000221353.44132.25

Roets, A., Kruglanski, A. W., Kossowska, M., Pierro, A., & Hong, Y. (2015). "The Motivated Gatekeeper of Our Minds." *Advances in Experimental Social Psychology,* 221–283. https://doi.org/10.1016/bs.aesp.2015.01.001

Life

YOU MAY BE ABLE TO REMAIN FRIENDS, BUT GIVE IT A MINUTE

So your ex is a solid good person, they just aren't *your* person anymore. Can you remain friends? Absolutely, for sure. But . . . you may need to give each other some space to do so. You are learning who you are when not with them, and that's important work that you don't want influenced so strongly by your past, right?

I wrote in my book *Unfuck Your Brain* about the trauma timeline and already referenced it earlier in the book. If you're skipping around a bit and didn't read that section yet, trauma research states it takes about ninety days for our brains to adjust and the first thirty are the most crucial to that process. And I think that's a solid amount of time to consider giving yourself.

Does the research on breakups correlate with that trauma research? There isn't much out there. If you've looked online recently, the one study that shows up time and again is the "eight year" study. Researchers measured emotional attachment and bonding to an ex. In this study, study participants had been with their former partner for at least two years (no three-week situationships, it had to be a long-term relationship), and they found that it takes on average about eight years to get over one's ex.

Except.

I don't know if that's exactly what they measured.

In the study, they measured responses to their ex-partner versus a stranger. It's no surprise that it takes a *very* long time for us to have the same lack of attachment to our ex than we would a complete stranger. And "emotional attachment" doesn't mean one is still grieving the relationship. It does mean this is someone you fucking knew very fucking well for a fucking good amount of time.

And, of course, you are going to respond to them differently than you would a stranger. Unless you have no contact with them for many years and they . . . become a stranger. The researchers who designed this study pointed out that it takes longer if you still have a level of contact with them. Well, yeah. And if the point is to maintain a friendship, you will still have an emotional attachment to them. Just a different one.

So it sounds like my therapist-y answer still stands.

It takes a few months to get used to your new normal. Go slowly with the friendship stuff until your brain is caught up with reality. You don't necessarily need to go no-contact, but think through what you want to know about and what you don't. What feels comfortable to talk about and what doesn't? Set boundaries and let your ex know if any conversation has too many sharp edges to undertake right now. If they really are a great person who's worth staying friends with? They will respect your needs as you adjust.

The Research

Chong, J. Y., & Fraley, R. C. (2025). "The Long-Term Stability of Affective Bonds After Romantic Separation: Do Attachments Simply Fade Away?" Social Psychological and Personality Science, 0(0). https://doi.org/10.1177/19485506251323624

Harper, F. G. (2017). Unfuck Your Brain. Microcosm Publishing.

GET SUPPORT FROM YOUR FRIENDS AND FAMILY. BUT NOT JUST YOUR FRIENDS AND FAMILY.

I had a client I worked with for some months who scheduled the first appointment because, as he said, he was going through some big relationship changes and didn't want to burn out his friends in the process. And that was the healthiest, most loving decision he could have made for both his friends and himself.

I was reminded of this recently when my son said he preferred talking to friends and family about his problems because we actually care, and therapists are only paid to care. He acknowledged how much I truly care about and love my clients but said that I'm an outlier. Am I an outlier? Nah. But is it also true that there are clinicians who don't give a SHIT?

Yeah, they exist, unfortunately. I'm so sorry if you have felt like your clinical support people didn't care about you in the past. They should. And this is exactly one of the situations where you need to know they care about you as a fellow person on the planet.

A breakup that you are struggling to make sense of? Where the grief and loss have been overwhelming with no relief in sight? This is exactly the time where working with a professional may really help you move toward healing. If things are this rough, you need supportive care. Let your friends be your friends. You need them to hang out with you and watch dumb movies and eat nachos . . . and you need your therapist to help you break out of the patterns that are keeping you trapped in grief instead of creating space around it.

And if you feel your therapist doesn't care about you or support you? Get another. And another. And another. Until you find your person. That doesn't mean they will agree with every rowdy thing your brain wants to think or that every unhinged grief impulse you have is a helpful behavior to engage in. It means they empathize while gently showing you other paths forward. Letting intrusive thoughts win could mean bangs . . . or it could mean jail time. You want to know they care enough about you to help you avoid both—or at least to go with the bangs instead of sugar-in-the-ex's-gas-tank. You are absolutely allowed to break up with a therapist who can't help you process your other breakup. You have breakup practice now, at least.

And even with your friends, consider who you are sharing your stories with. Are they the right person for it? Will they protect your privacy? Understand without judgment? They may be a wonderful friend in many other regards but are not able to do that. And that's ok. You don't order a milkshake from Home Depot, right? I mean you can. But it will likely go over as well as asking your fun friend to be your sad-feelings-space-holding friend. It's tough enough being let down when everything is going well . . . and things aren't going well. So be mindful of who really has your six in these situations.

Real-Life Advice

Don't stop talking about it! Share your grief, talk to friends, therapists, and anyone else who will listen. And highly prioritize self-care and re-engaging in things that you love that you may have fallen out of while in the relationship.

– Jessica Gibbons

EMOTIONAL OVERLOAD BREAK: THE POWER OF THE PAUSE

Shenpa is a term attributed to Tibetan Buddhism that is traditionally translated as "attachment" although Buddhist nun Pema Chödrön says that it better translates in modern English to "hooked." Or "stickiness" or even "trigger." All of which help us better understand the concept since we often think of the term attachment to mean a level of emotional caring about a situation.

And, of course, when the Buddha said attachments make us suffer, he didn't mean to forgo emotional caring. He meant to let go of the outcome. That is, give a shit and do your best, but there are so many factors out there that can impact your plans, you are going to be constantly butthurt if you are continuously hooked into situations wherein things are not working out the way you want and you are building a sense of resentment over this undesired outcome.

Any of my clients can tell you, we always operationalize a difference between disappointment and butthurt. Disappointment is the experience of not having what you hoped to have. Butthurt is operationalized as the emotional response that comes from not getting something that you had a sense of entitlement about receiving. Not everything works out. And our continuous insistence that it *should* work out is what keeps us hooked into untenable situations. And if we are hooked, we feel a deep need to act. To fix the problem. To unbreak something that is broken.

Even the most healthy breakup still has individuals who need to contend with what was broken. And that it cannot be unbroken. Chödrön likens shenpa to having scabies. The more you scratch at it, the more it itches. And then you have an open wound that cannot heal; instead, it causes continuous problems and complications. And then we look for anything that helps us temporarily feel better, because feeling the pain seems unbearable.

However, sitting with our pain and letting it tell us what we need to know is actually the most bearable option. The fight against pain is far more the problem than the pain itself. The pain dissipates when we shine a light on it. However, if we remain hooked into resistance it has just the nutrients it needs to stay alive and grow and continue to cause damage in your life.

Give yourself some time to sit in as safe and quiet a place as you can find. And once the pain presents, Chödrön suggests a set of reminders she terms "the four Rs."

Recognition: That is just, "Yep, I see it. I feel it. That's the itch. It's uncomfortable and I want to scratch at it."

Refraining: This is when we actively choose to not engage in our scratching habit. Afford yourself some grace and humor in this process if possible. Feeling irritated at yourself or even defensive makes it harder to refrain. If you think "Ok, yep . . . that's me trying to get on my bullshit and not today, Satan!" you are far more likely to be successful. Gentle always works better when building new habits.

Relaxing: This just means stop fighting the pain and let yourself experience it. The pain will poke around a bit but will eventually dissipate when you notice it without feeding it. In my book *Unfuck Your Brain*, I note the research that demonstrates that emotions are meant to last only 90 seconds in the brain. They dissipate quickly when we note them for the information they are, rather than something we have to become hooked into.

Resolving: This last step is just an internal reminder that we can continue this practice and work with our minds gently when our pain becomes itchy again. With time it will dissipate more and more and will eventually be a minor annoyance we can swat away with ease.

The Research

Chödrön, P. (2019). *Taking the Leap: Freeing Ourselves from Old Habits and Fears.* Shambhala.

Harper, F. G. (2017). *Unfuck Your Brain.* Microcosm Publishing.

THE ONLINE STUFF

Our online footprints, especially regarding social media, give us a whole other host of decisions to make after a breakup. We often "disconnect" from our now-ex (unfriend, unfollow, take a break, block, etc.), which is a complicated decision in its own right. But then . . . what else? This is what researchers have identified as breakup social dilemmas.

What about your mutuals? Your friends? Their family members you have a relationship with? Your engagement with them could be visible to your ex or spoken of to your ex.

What about digital memories? Photos or videos they have posted in the past that contain you? Rarely can you legally demand they remove them. (Now, revenge porn is its own problem, and many states have revenge porn laws so you may have some legal recourse around any materials in which the subject [you] had a reasonable expectation of privacy, like it wasn't filmed for public consumption.)

Some people leave social media entirely, at least for a while, which is something I can see great benefit in doing. Though you may want to tell people you're taking a social-media-overwhelm break and aren't-dead-yet as a pinned post.

Or let them wonder, if that's your kink.

In general, the research on the topic suggests that if you don't actively involve social media in your breakup, then you are far less likely to have a messy breakup. And if you and ex-boo's lives were pretty intertwined on social media, you can't do much about that now (ugh, I know).

And yes, this includes disclosing the breakup at all. What about that part?

Now putting aside participating in an online support group, especially one with closed enrollment, is a different thing. If you joined, say, a single parents group as part of your support network after breaking up with your kiddo's other parent and you discuss those struggles . . . that's an expected and invited interaction.

But on your general main page? That's a different disclosure to consider.

All studies show that most people disclose their breakups offline, not online. Meaning the people you want to know get the information, and it isn't anyone else's business. (We will talk about the fine art of IRL disclosure in another section.)

So a social media post such as this is referred to as *negatively valenced information* instead of the highly curated, Christmas-card-letter type content (omgggg everything is so great in my life, now purchase my diet tea). This refers not just to breakups but scary health information, struggles with suicidality, and the like.

What was super interesting to me about this study was how different age groups interacted around negatively valanced information. People over 40 (my fellow olds) are far less likely to share this type of information online. The "why" of that wasn't studied but presumably relates to growing up without such platforms.

(My specific generation, Xers, have a tendency to just go silent in general when the information is negatively valanced as part of our own feral cultural conditioning. Give us our clove cigarettes, our Lisa Loeb CD, and a bag of Taco Bell and we will re-emerge in a bit.)

That part isn't super surprising, but what part might be is that the 40-pluses are far more likely to respond to negatively valanced online information with concern and care. Research demonstrates that we tend to be more comfortable with those types of exposure, which at least correlates (if not causes) us to respond.

Again, no information on the why, but I'm guessing those of us with some decades of adulthood under our belts are the first to admit that this shit is hard. We can relate and commiserate . . . even if we don't want to talk about our own shit in the process. Now, just like every other group, we prefer in-person disclosure, but we are the most understanding of online disclosure.

Other researchers looked at what is termed the "Big 5" personality traits. They are openness to experience, conscientiousness, extroversion, agreeableness, and neuroticism (which is really just an older word for negative emotionality . . . a propensity toward anxiety disorders and mood disorders). Only two of them showed statistically significant correlation with posting online about a relationship breakup.

I would have guessed that individuals who score higher in extraversion and neuroticism would be the ones most likely to post—but I was half wrong. Yes, people with more emotional health issues are more likely to post online. But the next one surprised me. It was people with less openness to experience. The other three (including extroversion, which was my initial guess) didn't correlate at all.

Again no why, but it kinda makes sense with some more thought for the peeps who really struggle with change. That's also going to make a breakup harder for them, dispositionally. Someone who expects and embraces change is going to be more likely to see positives in the future. Someone struggling may search out support from more sources.

That being said, the researchers caution that social media disclosure doesn't *actually* seem to provide the sought-after community support. "Oh sweetie, I'm so sorry" as a post response may help us feel seen and validated but isn't the kind of support we really need to start healing. Seeking offline support from friends, family, mentor, known community leader, and/or (of course) a therapist? Far more likely to provide you that higher level of support.

The same researchers noted that many people don't have those in-person relationships available, and they suggest seeking out individual connections online (or one of the aforementioned online groups specific to your needs). A lot of people for a lot of reasons are really isolated. This is a situation where finding an online community of others going through the same thing allows a give and take—with both the vulnerability of information disclosure and with support. That makes it a conversation, and mutual aid, rather than announcement-and-response.

Real-Life Advice

One of my biggest problems was keeping up with my ex's socials. Even though I knew it was wrong and only hurting me, I couldn't stop myself. Someone once suggested I be more aware when I'm doing it, and I started being able to stop myself and ask, "Is this helping me right now?" and "What can I do instead that would help me more?" Ultimately, keeping tabs on them served no real purpose (other than feeding my spite) and only made me feel extra awful. My healing journey sort of began in earnest once I stopped. I haven't checked their socials in years and have no intention to start again.

—Scarlett

The Research

C.A. Goldberg, PLLC. (2024, December 17). *States with Revenge Porn Laws - C.A. Goldberg*. C.A. Goldberg. https://www.cagoldberglaw.com/resources/states-with-revenge-porn-laws/

Gershon, I. 2010. *The Breakup 2.0: Disconnecting over New Media.* Cornell University Press.

Haimson, I. L., Andalibi, N. Munmun De Choudhury, and Gillian R Hayes. 2018. "Relationship breakup disclosures and media ideologies on Facebook." New Media & Society 20, 5 (2018), 1931–1952.

Lukacs, V., & Quan-Haase, A. (2015). "Romantic breakups on Facebook: new scales for studying post-breakup behaviors, digital distress, and surveillance." *Information Communication & Society, 18*(5), 492–508. https://doi.org/10.1080/1369118x.2015.1008540

Medeiros, D. T. and Webb, L. M. 2019. "Remaining Facebook versus Face-to-Face Friends after a Romantic Breakup: Factors that Distinguish Those Who Do from Those Who Do Not." *International Journal of Interactive Communication Systems and Technologies* (IJICST) 9, 1 (2019), 1–16.

Moncur, W. Gibson, L. and Herron, D. (2016). "The role of digital technologies during relationship breakdowns." *Proceedings of the 19th ACM Conference on Computer-Supported Cooperative Work & Social Computing.* 371–382.

Saling, L. L., Cohen, D. B., & Cooper, D. (2019). "Not close enough for comfort: Facebook users eschew high intimacy negative disclosures." *Personality and Individual Differences,* 142, 103-109.

Tran, T. B. and Joormann, J. (2015). "The role of Facebook use in mediating the relation between rumination and adjustment after a relationship breakup." *Computers in Human Behavior* 49 (2015), 56–61.

Zhao, X. & Schwanda S.. V., & Cosley, D. (2012). It's complicated: How romantic partners use Facebook. Conference on Human Factors in Computing Systems - Proceedings. 10.1145/2207676.2207788. Zhang, R., Freeman, G., & McNeese, N. J. (2020). "Breakups on social media." *Companion Publication of the 2020 Conference on Computer Supported Cooperative Work and Social Computing,* 431–435. https://doi.org/10.1145/3406865.3418310

TELLING YOUR FRIENDS AND FAMILY

In a previous section we talked about online disclosure considerations. To summarize, the results of this small study found that people tend to be more comfortable disclosing highly intimate, negatively valenced information *offline*, rather than online. Both talking about their own breakups and hearing about other people's breakups.

So we are all in agreement: in person is better. And if not in person as close to a two-way conversation as you can get. Video, phone, direct message. Now we have to figure out who are the safe people with whom you can share your story. And? What aspects do you share?

You may find many a relationship expert who will caution you to be discrete in what you share. Hard agree. You don't need to sprinkle a bunch of mess on everyone. Even if your ex is doing it. Honestly, ESPECIALLY if your ex is doing it.

(It won't take long for everyone involved to realize who is being dramatic and who is quietly doing the hard work of moving on. Be the latter.)

But research does also show that having space to talk about our heartbreak is important to our healing. Researchers have found that those who are able to process what happened heal faster. Literally. The researchers tracked heart rate as a means of gauging nervous system response, and the individuals who had a chance to talk and process had a much calmer nervous system after being able to do so.

And in a follow-up study, researchers found that being able to speak somewhat negatively about your ex also helps the healing process. I say "somewhat negatively" because a whole-ass rant tends to keep us riled up, leaving our healing out of reach. But talking about the reasons for the breakup and the things about them you are not gonna miss does help.

The researchers theorize that being in a relationship requires a level of psychological intertwining that has to be untangled. And talking about the breakup allows us a level of (what they termed) *self-concept reorganization.*

Normal speak? We have to remember who we are apart from the relationship we were in. If we are not me-with-someone, how do we just be "me" again? This processing time is essentially a form of narrative therapy . . . and we are telling the story of our recovery and healing.

So share that stuff with someone who is truly trustworthy, who recognizes that we don't share other people's stories. And someone who will gently get you reoriented if you are spinning out too much. You may have a couple such people in your life. A grounded bestie, a wise family member, etc. If not, back to this: it's entirely ok for you to see a therapist for a session or three to do your breakup processing. It's not just entirely ok, it's actively encouraged.

So what does a healthy conversation look like? It's far less this:

> *Holy hell, they are such an asshole. They never wanted to leave the house, they were irritable and rude if they noticed me at all, the house was always a mess, and their hygiene was just as bad. They are such a shitbag!*

And far more this:

> *I finally had to throw in the towel. I suspect they are struggling with some clinical depression, and I offered to help them find care, but they aren't ready yet. Which is entirely their right. However, as badly as it's affecting their life, it's also taking a pretty significant toll on mine. I couldn't carry the both of us emotionally, and I had to call*

it for my own sanity. I hope they get the treatment they need when they are ready to do so, but I'm focusing on my own needs right now instead of theirs. And honestly, it does feel soooooo nice to only have to clean up after myself.

Both are honest, one is kinder and more balanced. Now, what if your ex is abusive and awful and shitty and generally embodies all that is wrong with the world? You can still be honest without going so hard on the details that you and the person you are telling get all fucked up and retraumatized. That would look something like:

They were physically violent with me for most of our relationship. They're dangerous and I'm remaining no-contact with them and appreciate you keeping my movements private for just that reason. I'm still worried for my safety and am going to need a lot of recovery time

This is a statement that doesn't hide anything that has happened and goes hard on firmly expressed boundaries. But what if your ex is shit-talking you and lying so hard you now have whiplash? You can stand up for yourself without being messy in return:

I am so sorry you were drawn into our breakup in such an uncomfortable way. I can tell you that what you are reporting they said about me are not true statements. I hope I can demonstrate that I am the type of person who wouldn't do such things and that is clear to those around me, but I can't prove a negative, and I am not interested in exhausting myself by trying to.

This is the classiest way of saying, "No the fuck I did not, and that is such a load of shit I am not even going to waste energy on it . . . and if you can't see that it is a load of shit I don't have the time or crayons to explain to you why."

I can also say that these people can be really good at rallying others in their determination to trash you so no one knows that they're the trash. And they will be able to fool some people forever. And these are the why-bother people. Nothing you say will convince them that your shit-ass ex is a shit-ass.

The good news, though, the majority of your mutuals will see the story fall apart pretty quickly. Especially when your response to everything is a resounding, "I'm not defending myself against something that fucking stupid" while being "apologetic" that your ex triangulated them into y'alls private decision.

Being misrepresented suuuuuucks. And those of us who grew up chronically misunderstood are even more desirous of correcting the record as soon as possible. It will be incredibly uncomfortable the first few times you respond thusly. But after a while you'll notice it feels sooooo much better to not be drawn into your ex's web of bullshit anymore. And freeing to see exactly which people around you are trustworthy and respectful of your privacy. Let the trash take itself out.

Also? As hard as it can be in certain circumstances, don't ask people to make an allegiance to you in a breakup. And tell people that explicitly. Being asked to choose sides sucks, and you will earn so many good-friend points by not expecting them to do so. But also? Clearly state your boundaries. That you don't want your moves shared with your ex. That you aren't comfortable being at the same events with them right now. Or forever. Whatever your safety and healing needs are.

Your friends may remove themselves from your ex's orbit on their own, especially if they realize they're abusive, egregiously shitty, lying their asses off, etc. But let them figure it out for themselves. If you are doing your best to make those around you comfortable and your ex is doing the complete opposite? Real ones will spot that shit a mile away and will align themselves accordingly.

Real-Life Advice

My bestie would pick me up, and we would get a snack and go sit in the park. It didn't matter what time of the day it was. We would sit in silence sometimes or she would look at me and say, "Talk to me, goose." It didn't matter if I raged or cried! She sat in silence. When I was done (more like exhausted) she would ask me simple questions . . . What are you going to do? How are you going to change? How are you going to move forward? Then she would tell me to *be* about it, not *talk* about it. I would moan and groan and give a million excuses . . . however, when I started being about it, things changed! I had therapy with a real licensed person and my bestie!

—Karen Lyons

The Research

Aeby, G., & van Hooff, J. (2019). "Who gets custody of the friends? Online narratives of changes in friendship networks following relationship breakdown." Families, Relationships and Societies, 8(3), 411-426. Retrieved Apr 9, 2025, from https://doi.org/10.1332/204674318X15271464535444

Langeslag, S. J. E., & Sanchez, M. E. (2018). "Down-regulation of love feelings after a romantic break-up: Self-report and electrophysiological data." Journal of Experimental Psychology: General, 147(5), 720–733. https://doi.org/10.1037/xge0000360

Larson, G. M., & Sbarra, D. A. (2015). "Participating in Research on Romantic Breakups Promotes Emotional Recovery via Changes in Self-Concept Clarity." Social Psychological and Personality Science, 6(4), 399-406. https://doi.org/10.1177/1948550614563085 (Original work published 2015)

BREAKUP SAFETY STRATEGIES

It pisses me off that we have grown so little as a society that we still have to talk about strategies to keep yourself safe if you are planning on/even considering breaking up with your romantic partner. But to write a book about breakups without being honest about safety concerns would be bullshit.

Interpersonal violence is a common denominator among all people. Doesn't matter your cultural background, your SES, your gender even. We are all at risk, and I want you to be able to reclaim your life from a bad relationship without more harm perpetuated against you.

Let's talk about intimate partner violence (IPV) statistics for a minute. In the US, 24 people are the victims of rape, physical violence, or stalking at the hands of an intimate partner *per minute.* That's 12 million people (not just women) every year. Also, 29 percent of women and 10 percent of men[1] were harmed enough by IPV to have it impact their functioning, and more than half of those individuals sustained a significant injury from IPV.

And that's physical violence. Coercive control (psychological aggression) is reported in even higher numbers (almost half of all men and women have experienced this from a partner in their lifetime). And, oftentimes, these behaviors are entirely legal. A few states have moved to recognize coercive control as a form of domestic violence, while a few others allow it for inclusion in protective order requests, family court proceedings, etc. But you still have to prove it.

In the meantime, victims of coercive control are five times more likely to be killed by their partner. Keep in mind that in 20 percent of domestic homicide cases, the homicide was the first act of physical violence. I first wrote about coercive control in my book *Unfuck Your Boundaries*, and I think it's so important to be aware of how that may creep into your life that I included as an appendix in this book. I also included a big ole list of hotlines and agencies that can help you get out and get out safely if you are ready to leave. And help you stay safely if you aren't ready to leave.

---

1 I didn't find any data regarding individuals who are nonbinary (bigender, agender, 2s, etc. etc.) specifically, although the cited NIH study does demonstrate higher rates of IPV for non-cis people as an overall group. So I think it's safe to presume that those numbers suck, too.

There are also a bunch of safety plan forms online (google "domestic violence safety plan" on a device from which it is safe to do so. Even if you can't print one out and fill it out for yourself, you can get some idea of some things you can do to increase your chance of remaining safe should you stay or go. And please do.

Let's not lose you, too.

The Research

Black, M.C., Basile, K.C., Breiding, M.J., Smith, S.G., Walters, M.L., Merrick, M.T., Chen, J., & Stevens, M.R. (2011). The National Intimate Partner and Sexual Violence Survey (NISVS): 2010 Summary Report. Atlanta, GA: National Center for Injury Prevention and Control, Centers for Disease Control and Prevention.

Crossman, K. A., & Hardesty, J. L. (2018). "Placing coercive control at the center: What are the processes of coercive control and what makes control coercive?" Psychology of Violence, 8(2), 196–206. https://doi.org/10.1037/vio0000094

Fontes, L. A. (2024, July 1). Coercive control laws in the US should cover these 10 areas. DomesticShelters.org. https://www.domesticshelters.org/articles/legal/USA-coercive-control-lawsPeitzmeier, S. M., Malik, M., Kattari, S. K., Marrow, E., Stephenson, R., Agénor, M., & Reisner, S. L. (2020). "Intimate Partner Violence in Transgender Populations: Systematic Review and Meta-analysis of Prevalence and Correlates." American Journal of Public Health, 110(9), e1–e14. https://doi.org/10.2105/AJPH.2020.305774

Stark, E., & Hester, M. (2019). "Coercive Control: Update and Review." Violence against Women,

25(1), 81-104. https://doi.org/10.1177/1077801218816191

US Department of Justice. (2003). Intimate Partner Homicide. https://www.ojp.gov/pdffiles1/jr000250.pdf

LEGAL ENTANGLEMENTS: DEALING WITH SHARED MONEY, STUFF, KIDS, PETS, HOME

I know, a breakup is hard enough. And now you got the state involved. And all the money that costs you.

I've done enough of what I've termed "divorce doula" counseling to tell you it doesn't have to be a shitshow. Because this area is NOT the place to weaponize our position with our ex. As I have said to many divorcing couples with children: "Someone has to act grown right now, so it might as well be the adults sitting in front of me."

If your ex-partner is unwilling to act grown? You stay grown anyway. Don't be a pushover but don't match that petty and shitty energy in return. Stand up for what's reasonable without burning shit to the ground in retaliation for their shady moves. It can take awhile for their shit to come back on them, but it almost always does.

A resource that you can search for online is the "Divorce Decisions Worksheet." The one I have cited below was created by helloDivorce, and it's a solid resource. For worksheets with more financial detail (less who is going to pick up the kiddos from soccer, more on who is going to pay for the cleats), check out the Institute for Divorce Financial Analysts.

I couldn't do near enough in one little section of one book to cover all you may need to cover. Fortunately, there are a ton of good tools to get you started and maybe even prevent you from having to spend a fortune to untangle your relationship ending.

Real-Life Advice

I think it is important to mute the person I just separated from. This ensures that I can check in on any messages or whatnot when I'm feeling up to it, and I don't have the pressure of phone notifications bugging me. I do this as it is not always possible to have a clean break entirely. When there are finances or children involved, going full no contact is simply not feasible. So I set a time and space to check on messages that may be relevant or important for the things that need sorting out and ignore the rest.

Literally—I will NOT respond to anything that does not have something to do with whatever entanglement we are working to sort out. I keep it civil, professional, and as detached as I can manage, often crowdsourcing responses before sending them. It helps me take back my power and ensure that I am able to achieve the steps needed for a safe breakup—without causing additional turmoil.

—Amber J.

The Research

Divorce decisions worksheet. (n.d.). https://20830915.fs1.hubspotusercontent-na1.net/hubfs/20830915/Downloads/Generic/Divorce%20101%20-%20Divorce%20Decisions%20Worksheet.pdf

Essential Divorce Checklists & Worksheets. IDFA. (n.d.). https://institutedfa.com/divorce-checklists-worksheets/

EMOTIONAL OVERLOAD BREAK: MEDITATION ON THE SOLES OF THE FEET

The fact that I am a big fan of meditation and mindfulness is pretty evident from other planets at this point. I learned about this particular version a few years ago in trauma training (also not a surprise) because researchers found that this particular meditation calms anger responses.

Anger is a secondary response, meaning it's an emotion that arises as a response to a need or want not being met. Grief and hurt definitely count. And this particular meditation is a somatic one: You are actively engaging in and building increased awareness of your body in the process.

The meditation is designed to let you feel your anger in a safe way in order to help it dissipate back into the ether.

And before you start, this may be a "well, duh" thing to say but the more calm and relaxing the atmosphere, the better. Even if you can just dim the lighting a bit it can really help.

1. If you are standing, stand in a natural rather than an aggressive posture.
2. If you are sitting, sit comfortably with the soles of your feet flat on the floor.
3. Breathe naturally and do nothing.
4. Cast your mind back to an incident that made you very angry. Stay with the anger.
5. You are feeling angry, and angry thoughts are flowing through your mind. Let them flow naturally, without restriction. Stay with the anger. Your body may show signs of anger (e.g., rapid breathing).
6. Now, shift all your attention to the soles of your feet.
7. Slowly, move your toes, feel your shoes covering your feet, feel the texture of your socks or hose, the curve of your arch, and the heels of your feet against the back of your shoes. If you do not have shoes on, feel the floor or carpet with the soles of your feet.
8. Keep breathing naturally and focus on the soles of your feet until you feel calm.

9. Meditate on the soles of your feet for about 10 to 15 minutes.
10. Slowly come out of your meditation, sit quietly for a few moments, and then resume your daily activities.

The Research

Singh, N. N., Lancioni, G. E., Winton, A. S., Adkins, A. D., Wahler, R. G., Sabaawi, M., & Singh, J. (2007). "Individuals with mental illness can control their aggressive behavior through mindfulness training." ***Behavior Modification, 31*****(3), 313–328. https://doi.org/10.1177/0145445506293585**

VRRR

NEVERENDING BREAKUPS

There are multiple surveys out there looking at how many people report having gotten back together with an ex. The numbers vary (which makes sense, cuz self-reported surveys tend to vary quite a bit), ranging from 21 to 44 percent.

So yeah, it is not-that-surprisingly common. You don't have to be Ben Affleck to have the urge.

Is it a good idea?

The research shows that these on-again relationships are qualitatively less than other (only-once) relationships. Rene Dailey, a relational communications researcher has published several studies that show that these on-again relational redos tend to be pretty mid.

She found in her research that back-together peeps report less relational satisfaction, feel less validation, less love, less sexual satisfaction, and less fulfillment of their needs.

Which? Well, yuck.

People get back together with their exes for any number of reasons. And whatever your reason for reconsideration? It's more than likely a commonly stated one. And no judgments about those thoughts and feelings. Loneliness is real. Still loving them is real. The overwhelm of the dating scene is real. Felt, felt, and felt.

But whatever led to the breakup will quite likely lead to yet another breakup if the underlying cause of the breakup isn't attended to. If both of y'all are doing some significant work and continue to address those issues that got you broken to begin with, then yes . . . you have a shot of making it work. Fix the shit you need to fix. While they are fixing the shit they need to fix. Then see where y'all are and how y'all feel.

Real-Life Advice

I wanted to get back together with them and felt like I needed them, and my therapist said, "The source of your troubles can't also be the solution" and that stuck with me.

—Korra

The Research

Dailey, R. M., Pfiester, A., Jin, B., Beck, G., & Clark, G. (2009). "On-again/off-again dating relationships: How are they different from other dating relationships?" *Personal Relationships, 16,* 23-47.

Dailey, R. M., Jin, B., Pfiester, A., & Beck, G. (2011). "On-again/off-again dating relationships: What keeps partners coming back?" *The Journal of Social Psychology,* 151(4), 417-440.

Dailey, R. M., & Powell, A. (2017). "Love, sex, and satisfaction in on-again/off-again relationships: Exploring what might make these relationships alluring." *Journal of Relationships Research.*

Gibson, T. (2025, March 10). "7 types of breakups that get back together." https://blog.personaldevelopmentschool.com/post/types-of-breakups-that-get-back-together

WATCHING YOUR EX THRIVE WITHOUT YOU

There was a meme going around recently that stated, essentially, when a couple breaks up, watch for who gets the glow up and who is still on their bullshit. That'll tell you who the problem was. And there is truth to that in many circumstances. I have seen many people of all genders truly blossom into their authentic selves after crawling out from under a harmful relationship.

It can also be the case in a mutual and mature breakup, however. Not because you were an awful burden on your ex but because you were both devoting so much time and energy to bailing water from the sinking boat you are both in, they have the time and space to finally bloom.

And you are on that same path, even if your timeline is different.

But, in the meantime, you are feeling grouchy and irritated and a little petty over their growth outpacing yours. And maybe even feeling like a booty-hole for begrudging them their happiness.

And that is where self compassion work comes into play. Reminding yourself that you are a messy human with messy emotions just like every other human on the planet, and this shit is just really difficult. And remind yourself that it's not a sprint. If you are putting in the difficult work of growth, I promise you will look up one day and realize you are firmly on the path you want to be on.

(Think of it like taking an aspirin for a headache. You don't recognize the moment the headache turns off, but at some point you realize it did. And you're feeling pretty ok again.)

The self-coaching when this is the situation is to remind yourself that you both gave each other an important gift. Freedom to be who you need to be. They are thriving because of it, and you are on that path, too. You can even say something to that effect if people point out how well ex is doing. As in responding:

I am so glad to hear that! We realized that as much as we love and admire each other, we weren't providing each other the kind of support we needed to be our full selves. The fact that they are doing so now was exactly the point. I'm on the same journey, and we will both look at our breakup as a difficult, necessary gift that we needed to give each other.

But maybe say it marginally less cheesily than I just did. And then remind yourself, with your inside thoughts, that this is intellectually true even if it isn't emotionally true at the moment. And that's ok. So long as we feel petty but don't act petty against someone who doesn't deserve it? That's enough.

But you know who else is good at really looking like they are happily in their lane, moisturized and unbothered? Assholes who manage to avoid consequences because they live at a surface level, while the partner they fucked over is doing the heavy lifting or real recovery work. And the partner whose energy was vampirically drained over months and years is working to just stop curling up in the fetal position in the corner while rocking back and forth.

Most anyone who has been on the dating streets long enough has invested time into that person and feels lucky to have escaped. And watching them bounce off to their next victim with zero consequences and zero self-reflection suuuuuuuuuucks.

And? (I am so sorry) The best thing you can do for yourself is let that shit go. Vent to your therapist about it and then process with them that people like that are very, very good at manipulating both other people and life circumstances. It takes way more time before those people finally FAFO and get their karma. It'll happen. And in the meantime, you're making the decision to live in a place of grief, healing, and growth. Which is a way better human endeavor than avoiding your work in pursuit of more bullshit.

The even better part? Whenever their FAFO gremlin strikes, and someone reports back to you that they are finally getting their comeuppance? You'll be relieved that they're no longer damaging others. And maybe a little amused at whatever circumstances finally knocked them on their ass. But mostly? You won't really care. Because you already crawled out of the hell hole they left you in. And none of their bullshit is your concern. And that is so fully the absolute best revenge.

Real-Life Advice

My friend gave me advice to imagine my life in the future, six months, one year, five years and how many changes will have happened and what opportunities I might have then because of the breakup that I wouldn't have if the relationship had continued.

—Kim

BE KINDER
BE A BETTER PARTNER
PRACTICE SELF-CARE
LIST

ASK YOUR FUTURE SELF ABOUT YOUR PRESENT BEHAVIOR

So this one isn't an evidence-based practice concept, but it is a practice-based evidence concept based on my practice as a therapist and coach. And it has come in super handy when working with people going through a breakup, especially a contentious one where there are issues to untangle around who owns what, who should get what from whom, who the kids and pets will be with, etc.

And I have had many people come back and tell me they were grateful for the following question:

Will you be embarrassed about this action looking back on it ten years from now?

This question is not about how we learn and grow from our mistakes. We can all look back at things we did in the past and be embarrassed because we didn't know any better back then. That's called growth, and thank fuck for it. This question asks, *Do you know better now?* Are you looking at a particular course of action (mean, vindictive, petty, etc.) because you are hurt and angry? Is it an action that is out of your moral alignment?

If I can recognize, "I'm looking at ways of being hurtful because I am hurt, and I know I'll be upset at myself about it later," I can talk myself off the Ledge of Petty and act right in the present. It's not as satisfying in the here and now, but future-you will be awfully grateful. Trust Auntie Faith.

Real-Life Advice

I tried on a lot of resentments. Bitterness. Anger. I did a lot of sobbing for the loss of the life I thought we would have and said we both wanted. I am a practicing witch so I cast several unbinding candle spells. In the end, detachment helped me the most.

—Blair F.

"You're doing a great job!"

BUT, HEY! POST-TRAUMATIC GROWTH IS ALSO A THING

I don't mean this in a spiritual bypassing "everything happens for a reason" kind of way.

And for what it's worth? Bad things happen because life is hard and shit is fucked sometimes. Not because the Universe thinks you in particular have some growth to do. Growth happens regardless.

So when we talk about post-traumatic growth, it's not with the idea that that was the point. Because I'm so incredibly sorry you had to go through a breakup and all the ensuing pain. But as we honor the pain, we can also honor the growth we gained in the experience as well. Multiple studies found that after a breakup, people reported increases in constructs like self-confidence, independence, emotional strength, and emotional stability.

These studies also found that people used the breakup as a motivator to improve their own well-being and make positive changes in how they approach future relationships, stating they feel they are now more skillful at communication and managing conflict.

And thank fuck for all that, right? It means we're learning to not make the same mistakes over and over again. And instead are saving our energy for new and different and more interesting mistakes. So pay attention to what you are learning and noticing here. The growth is the opportunity not to give the breakup some level of "meaning" but as a reminder that even in the worst shit, we have amazing capacity to both heal and take lessons learned into future relationships.

Real-Life Advice

Reinventing myself I think helped me pick up my pieces. I tried a lot of new hobbies, some of which I used for catharsis like writing erotica, but some just to be curious and try something new. Reconnecting with my curious spirit not only helped guide me to fun new endeavors I'm still carrying today but also taught me to question assumptions I'd been making about my ex and our breakup and brought me to better clarity.

—Scarlett

My mom always told me that when bad things happen, it is important to let yourself fall apart. Give yourself two weeks to fully fall into the sadness, and if you're not sick of yourself after three days you are doing it wrong, and it's time to get back up and start moving forward. She gave me this nugget of wisdom after my first boyfriend broke up with me and I, in my teenage earnestness, wasn't sure how I would ever recover from my three-month-long relationship. This advice has gotten me through many a breakup, breakdown, and all the political bullshit through the years.

—Amber J.

The Research

Kansky, J., & Allen, J. P. (2018). "Making Sense and Moving On: The Potential for Individual and Interpersonal Growth Following Emerging Adult Breakups." ***Emerging Adulthood (Print)*****, 6(3), 172–190. https://doi.org/10.1177/2167696817711766**

EMOTIONAL OVERLOAD BREAK: MEDITATION FOR SUFFERING

Tonglen is a Tibetan word that means take-give. Tonglen has traditionally been taught as just one of many practices in the tradition of Tibetan Lojong (mind-training) and is attributed to the famous Bengali teacher, Atisha (980-1054 CE). Which is to say, it's some medicine with some years behind its effectiveness. In fact it was considered a closed practice, for a very long time.

I was struggling greatly with grief when a friend who has also taken refuge in the Buddha suggested I practice tonglen.

I had previously used tonglen when sitting with someone who was dying but didn't admit it was because I needed something to do—with their pain, with my own at losing them. Being with dying sucks. Living with grief sucks. Tonglen became a grief practice for me because it didn't try to force any change in the nature of the pain. But sitting with it and attending to that pain with love and respect? The pain changed itself. The edges softened. It settled down. It didn't yell and scream and demand attention because it was being seen and heard and understood.

To do it, you breathe *in* the pain (your pain, the pain of others, the pain of the world) and breathe *out* healing energy on the behalf of all of us in pain. You could use it, I could use it. Hell, there are a lot of people around both of us who don't even know how much they could use it. Let's breathe tonglen for them, too. Maybe it'll help.

Wouldn't breathing in our own pain just mean we are mucking around in our shit again? Not if we do it right. Instead of holding it, we are recognizing it and giving it an opportunity to move, to soften, to release. Like dying, a breakup is a type of pain that needs to be sat with and heard.

Give it a try. Breathe in a mindfulness of your experience as a fundamentally human one, and breathe out a relief for both yourself and others feeling similar pain. What shifts inside you? How do you feel in relation to the rest of the world?

The Research

Pagliaro, G., Pandolfi, P., Collina, N., Frezza, G., Brandes, A., Galli, M., Avventuroso, F. M., De Lisio, S., Musti, M. A., Franceschi, E., Esposti, R. D., Lombardo, L., Cavallo, G., Di Battista, M., Rimondini, S., Poggi, R., Susini, C., Renzi, R., & Marconi, L. (2016). "A Randomized Controlled Trial of Tong Len Meditation Practice in Cancer Patients: Evaluation of a Distant Psychological Healing Effect." *Explore (New York, N.Y.), 12*(1), 42–49. https://doi.org/10.1016/j.explore.2015.10.001

FORMING NEW HEALING HABITS

Remember earlier when we talked about how the "21 days to change a habit" thing is bullshit? That's an even truthier-truth when we look at habit formation. The nature of a breakup, no matter how connected y'all's life was or wasn't, means some level of change. And if we are going to go through all this pain, doesn't it make sense that we change for the better? That we do things to make us happier and healthier?

Change, even for the better, is really hard to undertake. You'd think otherwise, right? Like if eating better makes you feel better, that should be an easier habit to maintain. Cuz we all prefer feeling better, unless you have a shame kink you didn't tell me about.

But you've also experienced the frustration of maintaining a new habit. Those gains are typically short-lived cuz human brains are so stubborn. Because we have to create new neural pathways around the behavior. In other words, doing dumb shit is easier for our brain to handle than smart shit if we are used to doing dumb shit. Enforcing a new habit is referred to as a System 2 process because we have to think about it. Doing something without thinking about it is a System 1 process.

One of the best ways to convert a System 2 process into a System 1 process is to maintain consistency in the habit by finding ways to make the new habit easier to engage in than the old one. Again, to use the science-y explanation, this means we need "built-in mechanisms for maintenance." So, if you are working on getting up and going for a walk in the morning instead of bed rotting for an hour while doom scrolling? You might sleep in your workout clothes and have your walking shoes right by the bed. Your old habit is to get up and start the coffee, but what if your water bottle and keys were sitting by the coffee pot practically yelling, "First we go move our body!!"? Far more likely to engage in that process until it becomes the thing you do without thinking.

The brain likes to do without thinking as much as possible (insert all relevant stupid human jokes here). But it isn't laziness, it's cognitive efficiency. It frees up our brains to focus on other relevant things. So as you look at building new habits that are reasonable and sustainable, look for ways to make them as easy or easier to engage in than the old habit.

You're doing all this work to be your best self, so do everything you can think of to set yourself up for success.

Real-Life Advice

I committed the time I would have spent with my ex engaging in exercise, reading, new hobbies, and connecting through volunteer opportunities.

—Patti T.

[After a breakup] I started to date myself. I take myself out to the bookstore or to get coffee. I go to a hairstylist for a blow out (to avoid getting bangs). I organize and rearrange a room, as I find it helps me declutter my thoughts, and give my environment a "new" look that helps me break from the old routine. I connect with loved ones and friends and ask for help. I'll see if they can get pizza with me or hang out once a week for a while. I do this especially because I feel like the only thing I want to do is hermit and be alone. That is my brain's signal that it is desperate for healthful connection, so I go against my "want" and lean into the "need" for connecting.

—Amber J.

The Research

Gardner, B., Lally, P., & Wardle, J. (2012). "Making health habitual: the psychology of 'habit-formation' and general practice." The British Journal of General Practice: the Journal of the Royal College of General Practitioners, 62(605), 664–666. https://doi.org/10.3399/bjgp12X659466

Kahneman, D. (2024). Thinking, Fast and Slow. Penguin Books.

"Is this okay?"

"Oh yes!"

REBOUNDS

A relationship that is referred to as a rebound is one that is understood to have been initiated shortly after breaking up with someone else, with the idea being that the needed resolution and healing one requires hasn't happened yet. For this reason, *rebound relationships* are almost universally considered a bad idea.

You need time for yourself. You need to grieve and heal. Anyone you end up dating during this nebulously defined period of healing is considered transitional rather than authentic. Meaning the relationship isn't real because the rebounder is in it for the wrong reasons.

This is conventional wisdom. That is, something generally accepted as fact. It is so widely believed that there was hardly any actual research on the topic. So in more recent years, researchers decided to see if conventional wisdom holds. Turns out? Nope.

(This is why I always return to the research. Feelings aren't facts, and I was wrong as hell for believing that rebound relationships are a terrible idea.)

In fact? It's pretty much just fucking fine. And being in a new relationship isn't correlated with negative experiences but *is* correlated with positive ones. People who started dating someone new soon after a breakup felt more confidence, a better sense of closure regarding the old relationship (more feelings of resolution and fewer feelings of preoccupation to be exact), and generally reported better psychological and relational health.

I know. I know! Because now we are wondering how long those rebound relationships lasted. Was it all well and good and then it fell apart really damn quick because all that hearts and flowers shit was just a way of avoiding reality? Turns out? Also no. The amount of time that people took between relationships did *not* have any predictive value on when the second relationship ended (for the ones that did).

And all of this? Had nothing to do with how good or bad the previous relationship was in terms of commitment, relational satisfaction, and emotional attachment. The only bit of data that popped up that made the rebounders seem a bit petty was that many people reported that dating someone new so quickly gave them a sense of revenge over the past partner. Which, yeah. Makes sense. Recognizing that someone else thinking you're great when your ex-partner didn't? This is a fair thing to notice and enjoy. Just don't hire a skywriter about it.

One study points out that men are far more likely to rebound quickly than women, with the data showing that it is far more common in men with lower social supports. That is, it's far more likely for men to not have emotionally supportive friends and family, relying on a romantic partner to provide this to them, driving them to a new relationship more quickly.

But, again, even with these reports of less-than-noble driving forces, the people involved had just as many positive outcomes as all their fellow rebounders.

So if the question is, should I wait? The answer is absolutely. If that's what feels right for you. If you want to date again right away? The answer to that is *also* absolutely. If that's what feels right for you. And feel free to show this research to anyone who is demonstrating concern for your decision to do so.

The Research

Brumbaugh, C. C., & Fraley, R. C. (2014). "Too fast, too soon? An empirical investigation into rebound relationships." Journal of Social and Personal

Relationships, 32(1), 99-118. https://doi.org/10.1177/0265407514525086 (Original work published 2015)

Lue N. (2012). "Rebound relationships in a nutshell: Transitionals, buffers and why you should step away from the light when they're not over their ex." Baggage Reclaim. Retrieved May 10, 2012, from http://www.baggagereclaim.co.uk/rebound-relationships-in-a-nutshell-transitionals-buffers-why-you-should-step-away-from-the-light-when-theyre-not-over-their-ex/

Shimek, C., & Bello, R. (2014). "Coping with Break-Ups: Rebound Relationships and Gender Socialization." Social Sciences, 3(1), 24-43. https://doi.org/10.3390/socsci3010024

Wang H., Amato P. R. (2000). "Predictors of divorce adjustment: Stressors, resources, and definitions." Journal of Marriage and the Family, 62, 655–668.

Wolfinger N. H. (2007). "Does the rebound effect exist? Time to remarriage and subsequent union stability." Journal of Divorce and Remarriage, 46, 9–20.

It's a Match!
You and BeauTie liked each other.
You can now send them a message on your phone.
CONTINUE

GETTING "BACK OUT THERE"

Now that we all officially know that rebound relationships aren't doomed and you can date again whenever you fucking want to, let's talk about *getting back out there.* This will likely include dating again, at least at some point but is also so much more than that.

We've discussed all the ways a breakup often affects multiple life domains. So does your healing. Think of the breakup itself, and all it entails, as a form of *liminal space.* A doorway from one life to your next. Now as you finish crossing the threshold, what do you want this life to look like?

What had you let go of in service of this relationship? That isn't a bad thing, no judgments implied. Everything in life has a trade off. Maybe you put off grad school because you were helping your former partner start a business. Maybe it's not that huge, but you now don't have anyone else to consider if you decide you want purple bedroom walls with hot pink velvet curtains (it meeeeee!).

This is your time to reconnect with people you have seen less. And make new friends. And try new places. And take fun classes. Cook interesting shit. Start a garden. Adopt a stray cat or three (also meeeeeee!).

And make a plan. Like a for-real plan. It's easy to get stuck on ideas with no follow-through. And it can be of huge benefit to create a structure to your schedule, especially right now. Put your "back out there" plans on the calendar just as you would a dentist appointment. And you probably need to make a dentist appointment, too, right?

And have accountability partners for that matter. You used to do brunch with your ex on long weekends? Now you go hiking with your bestie. Or hit all your local bookshops. Ask the people who love you to show up for you.

And figure out you again. Not you-in-relation-to-a-partner. Just you.

Real-Life Advice

My therapist, who I established with soon after the separation, advised me to have self-care, stay active, and live with my feelings as well as allow myself to grieve. Wish I had started with her two years before. Exercise, quiet alone time, and continued working and being active as well as much research on anger, grief, depression, anxiety. I wish I got help with that long before, rather than trying to do it my damn self.

—Wayne

CONCLUSION

It's probably pretty evident at this point that I am not a fan of platitudes. Like the official definition of the term, they are oft-repeated moral messages that are not interesting or thoughtful. They also tend to not be factual. At least in any ways that suggest depth.

So none of that. Because ew.

Breakups suck. They just suck, and you're allowed to name it and claim it as sucking. You're allowed to grieve. You're allowed to take time to process and figure out what comes next. And THEN. When you (and only you!) are ready . . . you get to go embrace whatever it is that comes next.

Just keep an eye out for the cat distribution system. It'll sneak up on ya.

APPENDIX ONE: COERCIVE CONTROL

As mentioned earlier in this book, a form of abuse that is legal in most states and hard to prove in all of them is a strategic application of boundary violations as a means of controlling another human being.

Coercive control refers to regular patterns of boundary violating behaviors that create fear-based compliance in someone. The term was coined by Evan Stark whose 2007 book has the same name. His work brought to light how another person's systemic, organized boundary violations create an ongoing pattern of behavior that takes away our freedom of choice and ability to define our own personhood.

Dr. Stark's research shows that coercive control is present in up to 80 percent of abusive relationships. Which means only 20 percent of abusive relationships are defined purely by physical violence. Because it isn't something that is measured effectively (when it is measured at all), it is impossible to guess the number of relationships within the general population in which one partner abuses the other through these patterns of coercion.

Coercive control behaviors are not just a more extreme version of high conflict personality behaviors. High conflict responses are often the result of people perceiving their lives as out of control, and they perceive conflict as their best means of regaining control. It *is* a boundary-busting behavior, and those of us who are more empathic can end up feeling attacked and manipulated by high conflict, but that's not the end goal of the person engaging in conflict.

Coercive control, by contrast, is strategic, rational, and ongoing . . . not reactive in the heat of the moment. Individuals who engage in coercive control are seeking the measurable material and social benefits they can achieve by shattering the psyche of another person in order to own them.

And because mind-games, degradation, isolation, intimidation, regulation, and an ever-changing "rule book" are not illegal actions, they are even more effective at holding another human being hostage than inflicting physical pain. It's not the physical abuse, it's the mind-fuck. It's emotional terrorism. And it's the real reason it's so hard to leave an abusive partner. And the reason that so many abuse survivors suffer from PTSD.

Once physical and sexual intimate partner violence started to become socially unacceptable in the 1970s, individuals who abuse had to find other ways to maintain control over their victims . . . the uptick in coercive control in the past few decades correlates strongly with an uptick in legal consequences for perpetrating physical and sexual harm on a partner.

Dr. Stark notes that coercive control is steeped in gender-based privilege (and in case you are wondering, he is a cis/het dude); therefore, the focus of his work was on cisgender, heterosexual relationships in which men used coercive control techniques against their female partners. He notes that women are more vulnerable to coercive control because of their unequal political and economic status, which allows cis men to systematically take advantage of us at greater levels. Which means we are again hitting how insidiously *normal* rape culture is.

The numbers in this regard don't lie, but in my experience as a therapist, I can absolutely attest to how coercive control extends beyond this narrow definition. Coercive control exists within all manner of intimate relationships, in LGBTQ+ communities, among family members, within friendship groups, and within employer-employee relationships.

The common denominator of *unequal status* still applies to the dynamic of controller and controlled. Those with less power are far more susceptible to oppressive behavior by others whom they rely on for food, shelter, financial support, and/or safety.

How do these dynamics get created? It's a systematic, conscious process. Living in a society that centers power-over dynamics allows and even encourages means of owning the bodies and spirits of others. While most of us do not engage in that level of abusive power, there are plenty of people who do. There is a predisposition component (nature) to being a CC person, but it is far more a learned behavior (nurture). When people realize that they can perpetuate this kind of harm over another without consequence, they continue to do so.

A controlling individual sets the stage by cutting off their victim's means of support from the beginning. They seek out individuals who have vulnerabilities they can exploit. This may be people who are marginalized in significant ways (being poor, undocumented, isolated, etc.) or people who have the kind of abuse histories that have created permeable boundaries that the controlling individual can subvert almost immediately.

They set themselves up to become a rescuer in some fashion and create an indebtedness in their disempowered victim. They may rescue them financially from a bad situation. Or love bomb them with showered attention and care when they are at a low point and desperate for affection. They tether the vulnerable partner by ensuring more and more attachments to them and fewer attachments to others. At this point, resistance is worn down instead of strong-armed away.

Listed below are some of the more overt signs of being under the control of a coercive person, as well as some early-stage red flags to watch for. If you recognize yourself living these patterns, do know that there is support for getting out of an abusive situation. Even if they have never hurt you physically, domestic violence agencies can help you strategize a plan to leave safely (or stay safely, if that is your best option currently).

Signs of a coercively controlling person

When listed on paper, these activities seem pretty obvious, but when you are living this experience they sneak up in such a manner that we don't always see it until we step back.

The items on this list are based on the items used by researchers to measure coercive control in romantic partnerships:

- Controls/limits your contact with others (friends, family members, etc.) for instance by phone, internet, or chat.
- Wants all your passwords and access to all your accounts (but you don't have access to theirs)

- Tracks your movements through your cell phone (for your "safety")
- Makes demands regarding your movements (where you go, when you go, who you go with)
- Has physically stopped you from going somewhere or leaving the house (doesn't have to be by laying hands on you—they could block your exit, hide your keys, etc.)
- Spies on you/stalks you to check in on your movements
- Checks your clothes/receipts/items in the home for signs of your activities
- Audio or video tapes you either without your consent or by threatening you into consenting
- Asks others about your activities (your children, family members, friends, neighbors)
- Makes demands about your appearance (that you look or dress a certain way for them or maintain a certain weight)
- Controls household resources (bank accounts, vehicles, use of jointly produced income)
- Controls access to medical care

- Demands sexual intimacy in general, or specific sexual acts (either with them or with others on their demand)
- Controls use of contraceptives or STI prevention methods
- Interferes with or threatens your immigration/ citizenship status
- Creates other legal trouble for you
- Threatens your housing stability (e.g., threatening to kick you out of a home they pay for, breaking rules set in a home rental to have your lease terminated and get you both evicted)
- Controls all parenting decisions and parenting tasks
- Threatens harm
- Displays physical violence towards others or property to frighten you (punching walls, hurting a family pet)
- Otherwise scares you into submission
- Threatens self-harm in retaliation for your behaviors
- Engages in self-harm in retaliation for your behaviors
- Keeps you from work/makes you late to work/disrupts your workday/gets you fired
- Destroys your property

- Destroys the property of your friends and family
- Keeps weapons and makes threats (overt or veiled) to use them against you or someone else

Red flags of a manipulative partner or early stage coercively controlling partner

Along with the above, more overt behaviors, there are a lot of practices I see that also serve to wield power over another human being. These could be early warning sign behaviors in a new relationship that may become more intense as time goes on, or they could be occurring in longer-term relationships indicating a problem with systemic boundary violations. These behaviors are more belittling than controlling, but when done in a systematic way can invoke the process of wearing down resistance we see in coercively controlling relationships.

- Rude or dismissive of your friends and family
- Does not want you doing things with friends or family without their presence
- Excuses all their behavior rather than accepting accountability
- Needs constant contact with you through the day

- Engages in behaviors outside your value system and expects you to excuse them as "no big deal" or "jokes" (such as racial comments)
- "Jokes" about your appearance, passions, intelligence, culture, gender, or identity
- Challenges your worldview, motives, etc. consistently (rather than asking to better understand them)
- Otherwise does not support your values and passions
- Picks fights so you feel obligated to make things up to them
- Always expects you to wait for their attention, doesn't value your time
- Never admits any fault in past relationships ending
- Expects you to be okay with their behavior when it's not okay for you to engage in same-said behavior
- Is rude to people they see as beneath them (service workers, waitstaff)
- Minimizes your feelings and dismisses how their choices and behaviors affect you in negative ways (such as accusing you of being too sensitive)
- Frames your disagreement as you not understanding or listening to them effectively

- Questions your judgment ("Oh, you're wearing that?")
- Challenges or belittles your decisions, even decisions with little consequence
- Threatens you with social embarrassment
- Disrupts the well-being of other people in your life in order to disrupt your well-being (your children, family members, loved ones)
- Makes you responsible for their happiness, stability, contentment
- Is jealous of attention you pay to others

Coercive control strategies wielded toward lesbian, gay, plurisexual, trans, and nonbinary individuals

This list of power and control tactics is created by FORGE Forward, a website with a ton of great resources for trans people. I have found that many items on the list apply to relationships in which at least one person is not heterosexual, even if they are cisgender. Their list, with my additions based on my clinical experiences and the experiences of my friends, is below:

- Disregarding, diminishing, disrespecting your identity (names, pronouns, etc.)

- Making fun of or belittling these same identity markers
- Ridiculing your appearance
- Denying your identity (that you are not a real man, woman, enby, etc.)
- Using pejorative terms to describe your identity or aspects of your identity (including terms for body parts)
- Telling you no one will love you
- Telling you you are an embarrassment to communities to which you belong (LGBT community, church community, your bowling league, etc.)
- Refusing to let you discuss issues specific to your identity
- Threatening to out you to individuals you are not yet out to
- Weaponizing others' negative feelings about you to hurt you (e.g., having a fundamentalist preacher try to "save" you)
- Weaponizing the healthcare system or judicial system against you (threatening mental health commitments, police action, etc.)
- Restricting or denying access to medical affirmative care (therapy, hormones, surgery)

- Restricting or denying access to personal affirmative items (clothing, prosthetics, etc.)
- Fetishizing your body

Is coercive control a "fixable" thing?

Most people who set out to control others don't want to change; in these cases, it's much more important to focus on the safety of the victim. But that's not the case universally. Research demonstrates that when individuals experience therapeutic support that focuses on establishing equality and appropriate boundaries in relationships, along with behavioral strategies to manage violence and systematic desire to control, they can stop treating other people this way for good.

In fact, research shows that this type of support works better than incarceration for preventing future violence. Which makes total sense: the prison system is generally designed to perpetuate power-over models and reward power-over ways of thinking. The model developed by Ellen Pence in Minnesota, the Domestic Abuse Intervention Project, has demonstrated high success rates and is now used across the country.

There are also therapists who do this work in solo practice. You can search for offender treatment providers in your area, or call your rape crisis center and ask for clinician referrals.

And yes. I have worked with individuals who saw these red flags in themselves and wanted to unpack the histories that led them to this behavior, so they could make different and better choices in the future. And I have seen them go on to have healthy relationships. We can't go back and change our pasts, but we can make a conscious decision to say this behavior stops here and now, and make significant changes.

The big indicator of success in changing abusive behavior was that the coercively controlling individual had self-awareness of what they were doing and wanted to make that change. So if you see these red flags in your own behavior and are realizing that you want to change? That level of introspection is bad-ass. You will likely need support in making some serious changes in your relationships. But having healthy, fear-free relationships in the future will be well worth the effort.

And for those of us healing from those who violated our boundaries? Who are saying they're going to change if only you stick around? You don't have to do that. In fact, I generally encourage people not to. If they do the work, they have to do it for themselves . . . not in a panic because they want to keep someone around. It's fully ok to say, "I'm glad you're ready to do the work, us not being together will give you the time to do that. I'm really proud of you, best of luck! If they come back after some months or a year or so and want to discuss the changes they've made and how they would like to try again, you can decide THEN that it might be worth a shot or not.

APPENDIX TWO: RESOURCES RELATED TO INTERPERSONAL VIOLENCE

Resources for Victims and Survivors of Interpersonal Violence

The National Domestic Violence Hotline – 1-800-799-7233 (SAFE) – www.ndvh.org

Speak to (or message) an advocate to seek immediate help, gain resources for survivors, or to discuss your options for leaving, should you choose to do so.

National Dating Abuse Helpline – 1-866-331-9474 – www.loveisrespect.org

Find ways to prevent or end an abusive relationship. This hotline is tailored to young people but offers resources for concerned friends and family, as well.

National Sexual Assault Hotline – 1-800-656-4673 (HOPE) – www.rainn.org

Provides strategies for prevention and safety as well as healing and recovery.

National Suicide Prevention Lifeline – 1-800-273-8255 (TALK) – www.suicidepreventionlifeline.org

Offers support to those in distress or crisis, and provides prevention resources for loved ones.

National Center for Victims of Crime – 1-855-484-2846 (VICTIM) – www.victimsofcrime.org

Comprehensive advocacy program that helps victims of crimes rebuild their lives.

National Human Trafficking Resource Center/Polaris Project – Call: 1-888-373-7888 – Text: HELP to BeFree (233733) – www.polarisproject.org

Call (or text) for crisis assistance, survivor support, or to report possible trafficking. This hotline can also connect you with local anti-trafficking services in your area.

National Network for Immigrant and Refugee Rights – 1-510-465-1984 – www.nnirr.org

An organization whose mission is to defend and expand rights for immigrants and refugees. Call for resources, and get connected to local allies.

National Coalition for the Homeless – 1-202-737-6444 – www.nationalhomeless.org

Network of advocacy groups working to prevent and end homelessness. Call to get emergency assistance from your local service providers.

National Resource Center on Domestic Violence – 1-800-537-2238 – www.nrcdv.org and www.vawnet.org

Call to request individualized and comprehensive technical assistance and resources on intervention and prevention strategies.

National Center on Domestic Violence, Trauma & Mental Health – 1-312-726-7020 ext. 2011 – www.nationalcenterdvtraumamh.org

Offers assistance, resources, and training to advocates and service providers working with survivors.

Resources Specific to Children

Childhelp USA/National Child Abuse Hotline – 1-800-422-4453 – www.childhelpusa.org

Call to get help in reporting child abuse or to speak to a Childhelp counselor.

Children's Defense Fund – 202-628-8787 – www.childrensdefense.org

A non-profit child advocacy program that lobbies for the rights of all children in America, particularly poor children, children of color and those with disabilities.

Child Welfare League of America – 202-688-4200 – www.cwla.org

Coalition of private and public agencies dedicated to serving vulnerable children and families

National Council on Juvenile and Family Court Judges – 775-507-4777 – www.ncjfcj.org

Child Protection and custody/resource center on domestic violence, which can benefit individuals who have been victims of coercive control.

Center for Judicial Excellence – 415-444-6556 – www.centerforjudicialexcellence.org

Nonprofit organization focused on creating judicial accountability in the family court system, their focus on policy change is a fantastic resource for individuals who have found that their experiences of coercive control were not considered crimes by the court system.

Resources Specific to Teens

Love Is Respect – Hotline: 1-866-331-9474 or Text: LOVEIS to 22522 – www.loveisrespect.org

In association with the National Domestic Violence Hotline, this organization works to empower young people to prevent and end abusive relationships.

Break the Cycle – 202-849-6289 – www.breakthecycle.org

Organization centered around helping young people ages 12-24 build healthy and safe relationships.

Resource Specific to Deaf Women

Deaf Abused Women's Network (DAWN) – hotline@deafdawn.org – VP: 202-559-5366 – www.deafdawn.org

Agency that provides crisis intervention and survivor services for the Deaf, Hard of Hearing, and DeafBlind communities.

Resources Specific to Women of Color

Women of Color Network – 844-962-6462 – www.wocninc.org

A group established to address challenges facing Women of Color within the violence against women movement.

INCITE! Women of Color Against Violence – incite.natl@gmail.com – www.incite-national.org

Feminists of Color united to end state and domestic violence.

Resources to Specific to Latinx Individuals

Casa de Esperanza – Linea de crisis 24-horas/24-hour crisis line – 1-651-772-1611 – www.casadeesperanza.org

A bilingual domestic violence hotline. Their mission is to mobilize Latin@ communities to end domestic violence.

National Latin@ Network for Healthy Families and Communities – 1-651-646-5553 – www.nationallatinonetwork.org

Focuses on ending and preventing domestic violence in Latin@ communities, provides everything from shelter services to community engagement projects.

Resource Specific to Indigenous Women

National Indigenous Women's Resource Center – 855-649-7299 – www.niwrc.org

Organization dedicated to ending violence amongst native and indigenous populations through education and policy development.

Resources Specific to Asian and Pacific Islander Individuals

Asian and Pacific Islander Institute on Domestic Violence – 415-568-3315 – www.apiidv.org

Resource center for Asian and Pacific Islander communities facing issues of domestic violence.

Committee Against Anti-Asian Violence (CAAAV) – 1-212-473-6485 – www.caaav.org

Committee centered around organizing Asian communities to fight for institutional change.

Manavi – 1-732-435-1414 – www.manavi.org

Meeting needs (both immediate and long-term) for South Asian Women affected by violence.

Resource Specific to African-American Individuals

National Center on Violence Against Women in the Black Community – 1-844-778-5462 – ujimacommunity.org

Provides resources to and advocates for the Black Community in response to domestic, sexual, and community violence.

Resources Specific to Lesbian, Gay, Plurisexual, Trans, and NonBinary Individuals

The Audre Lorde Project – 1-718-596-0342 – www.alp.org

Organization working towards community wellness and social/economic justice for Lesbian, Gay, Bisexual, Two-Spirit, Trans and Gender Non Conforming People of Color.

LGBT National Help Center – 1-206-350-4283 – www.glnh.org

Provides peer support and local resources to the LGBT community.

National Gay and Lesbian Task Force – 1-202-393-5177 – www.ngltf.org

Organization focused on advancing justice and equality for LGBTQ people.

Northwest Network of Bisexual, Trans, Lesbian & Gay Survivors of Abuse – 1-206-568-7777 – www.nwnetwork.org

Network offering direct resources for victims of abuse, as well as resources for advocacy organizations.

Trans Lifeline – 877-565-8860 – www.translifeline.org

A hotline dedicated to improving the quality of trans lives and ending the epidemic of trans suicide by offering justice-oriented community aid.

Trevor Project – 1-866-488-7386 – thetrevorproject.org

Focused on preventing suicide and crisis intervention for LGBTQ and questioning individuals. The hotline is dedicated to helping those in need of immediate help.

It Gets Better – info@itgetsbetter.org – itgetsbetter.org

Aiming to uplift, empower and connect LGBTQ youth around the world.

Resource Specific to Older Adults

National Clearinghouse on Abuse in Later Life – 1-608-255-0539 – www.ncall.us

Provides technical assistance, training, and resources in order to advocate for elderly victims of abuse.

Resource Specific to Men

1in6 – 1in6.org

Provides men affected by sexual abuse or assault with survivor's resources.

Legal Resources

Battered Women's Justice Project – 1-800-903-0111 – www.bwjp.org

National resource center on civil and criminal justice responses to intimate partner violence.

Legal Momentum – 1-212-925-6635 – legalmomentum.org

Provides expert legal council in order to ensure economic and personal security for women and girls.

WomensLaw.org – www.womenslaw.org

Provides relevant legal information for all genders in regards to domestic and sexual violence.

National Clearinghouse for the Defense of Battered Women – 1-800-903-0111 x 3 – www.ncdbw.org

Provides customized technical assistance to victims of battery who are facing criminal charges or serving prison sentences.

Legal Network for Gender Equity – (202) 588-5180 – nwlc.org/join-the-legal-network/

Seeks gender justice in a variety of ways; in courtrooms, through public policies and cultural changes.

Resources Specific to Violence Prevention

National Organization for Men Against Sexism (NOMAS) – 1-720-466-3882 – www.nomas.org

A Call to Men – 1-917-922-6738 – www.acalltomen.org

Men Can Stop Rape – 1-202-265-6530 – mencanstoprape.org

Men Stopping Violence – 1-866-717-9317 – www.menstoppingviolence.org

ABOUT THE AUTHOR

Dr. Faith G. Harper, ACS, ACN, holds postdoctoral certifications in sexology and applied clinical nutrition and is trained in yoga, meditation, breathwork, mindful movement, and all of those other forms of care that make most people avoid her at parties. In the past, she has worked in academia, community mental health, and private practice as a licensed professional counselor. She maintains a connection with academia through her work with the Society of Indian Psychologists. She lives in San Antonio, TX, with her amazing friends and family and terrible rescue cats. She can be reached through her website, faithgharper.com.

MORE BY DR. FAITH

Books

The Autism Partner Handbook (with Joe Biel and Elly Blue)

The Autism Relationships Handbook (with Joe Biel)

Befriend Your Brain

Coping Skills

How to Be Accountable (with Joe Biel)

This Is Your Brain on Depression

Unfuck Your Addiction

Unfuck Your Adulting

Unfuck Your Anger

Unfuck Your Anxiety

Unfuck Your Blow Jobs

Unfuck Your Body

Unfuck Your Boundaries

Unfuck Your Brain

Unfuck Your Cunnilingus

Unfuck Your Friendships

Unfuck Your Grief

Unfuck Your Intimacy

Unfuck Your Stress

Unfuck Your Worth

Unfuck Your Writing (with Joe Biel)

Woke Parenting (with Bonnie Scott)

Workbooks

Achieve Your Goals

The Autism Relationships Workbook (with Joe Biel)

How to Be Accountable Workbook (with Joe Biel)

Unfuck Your Anger Workbook

Unfuck Your Anxiety Workbook

Unfuck Your Body Workbook

Unfuck Your Boundaries Workbook

Unfuck Your Intimacy Workbook

Unfuck Your Worth Workbook

Unfuck Your Year

Zines

The Autism Handbook (with Joe Biel)

BDSM FAQ

Dating

Defriending

Detox Your Masculinity (with Aaron Sapp)

Emotional Freedom Technique

Getting Over It

How to Find a Therapist

How to Say No

Indigenous Noms

Relationshipping

The Revolution Won't Forget the Holidays

Self-Compassion

Sex Tools

Sexing Yourself

STI FAQ (with Aaron Sapp)

Surviving

This Is Your Brain on Addiction

This Is Your Brain on Grief

This Is Your Brain on PTSD

Unfuck Your Consent

Unfuck Your Forgiveness

Unfuck Your Mental Health Paradigm

Unfuck Your Sleep

Unfuck Your Work

Vision Boarding

Woke Parenting #1–6 (with Bonnie Scott)

Other

Boundaries Conversation Deck

Stress Coping Skills Deck

How Do You Feel Today? (poster)